Rhyming
and Spelling
Dictionary

Pie Corbett ☆ Ruth Thomson

Contents

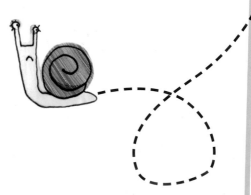

Using a rhyming dictionary

Rhymes are everywhere – in greetings cards, in playground games, chanted at football matches, in pop songs... and in many poems.

This rhyming dictionary makes it easier to write a rhyme. It can trigger all sorts of unusual rhyming words. Who would have thought of a chimpanzee smelling a sweet pea? Or of trying to hypnotize in pigsties!

Try flicking through the book for ideas for funny jingles and nonsense rhymes. It will also help you if you are stuck for a rhyme in a serious poem.

Rhyming and spelling

When words rhyme they share the same sound at the end, for example, fig and big. Not all words that rhyme share the same spelling patterns.

In this book you will find rhyming words which are spelled in different ways, although the end part sounds the same. For instance, there are nine different ways to spell the rhyming sound at the end of the word igloo: grew, ewe, two, shoe, you, through, flu, blue.

Poets look at words carefully and use rhymes to create images and make us laugh. As they build up a bank of words which rhyme, they come to know the various possibilities when spelling words. If you keep dipping into this book to create rhymes, it will help your spelling as well.

So what are you waiting for?
Open up this rhyming store.

Who's that on your mobile phone –
a fishbone or an ice cream cone?
Invent yourself a vagabond
and madly wave a magic wand.
Catch yourself a carnivore
dressed up in a pinafore!

Then post your rhyme to a friend –
rhyming words are cool to send...

How to find rhyming words

Use the page headings

★ This dictionary arranges words alphabetically according to their end vowel sounds: a, e, i, o or u.

★ To find words that end with a particular sound, first find the vowel sound (a, e, i, o or u) in the coloured strip at the top of the page, then look for the sound ending, e.g. –ay.

Use the index

★ The index lists words in alphabetical order. To find rhymes for a particular word, first look up that word in the index.

★ If you look up a word such as play, you will find it with a vowel sound after it and a page number: play / –ay 27.

★ On page 27 (see below) is a list of rhyming words with –ay sounds. The list starts with the shortest words and ends with the longest. You can use any of these words to rhyme with play.

★ Other sounds which rhyme with play, but which are spelled differently, are also listed, for example, neigh, prey and ballet.

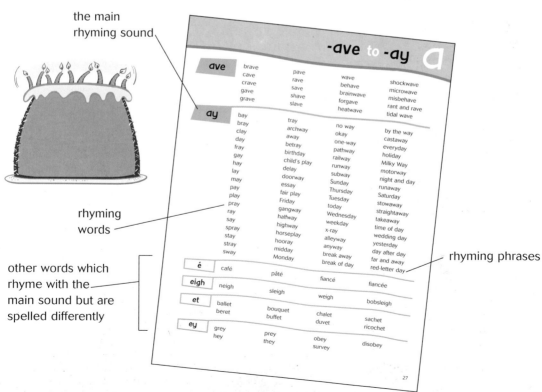

the main rhyming sound

rhyming words

other words which rhyme with the main sound but are spelled differently

rhyming phrases

-ave to -ay

ave
brave, cave, crave, gave, grave, pave, rave, save, shave, slave, wave, behave, brainwave, forgave, heatwave, shockwave, microwave, misbehave, rant and rave, tidal wave

ay
bay, bray, clay, day, fray, gay, hay, lay, may, pay, play, pray, ray, say, spray, stay, stray, sway, tray, archway, away, betray, birthday, child's play, delay, doorway, essay, fair play, Friday, gangway, halfway, highway, horseplay, hooray, midday, Monday, no way, okay, one-way, pathway, railway, runway, subway, Sunday, Thursday, Tuesday, today, Wednesday, weekday, x-ray, alleyway, anyway, break away, break of day, by the way, castaway, everyday, holiday, Milky Way, motorway, night and day, runaway, Saturday, stowaway, straightaway, takeaway, time of day, wedding day, yesterday, day after day, far and away, red-letter day

é
café, pâté, fiancé, fiancée

eigh
neigh, sleigh, weigh, bobsleigh

et
ballet, beret, bouquet, buffet, chalet, duvet, sachet, ricochet

ey
grey, hey, prey, they, obey, survey, disobey

27

5

Writing poetry

How to create sounds

Many poems use **full rhymes**. These are words which have exactly the same end sound, e.g. sm**ack** and bl**ack**. Some words nearly rhyme and these are called **near rhymes** or **half rhymes**, e.g. sl**ip** and s**leep**. Some words look as if they will rhyme, but actually do not. These are called **eye rhymes**, e.g. c**ough** and thr**ough**.

In most poems, the rhymes come at the *end* of the line:

Humpty Dumpty sat on a w**all**. Humpty Dumpty had a great f**all**.

Some poems use **internal** rhymes. These come in the *middle* of lines:

The sun sp**ills** sunlight, f**ills** corners with honey…

Rhymes help to bind a poem together and make sentences memorable. You can also use **alliteration** so that words start with the same sound:

The **s**un **s**pills **s**unlight…

Using words which sound like their meaning can make a poem really effective. This is called **onomatopoeia**:

The snake hissed.

How to create pictures

You can build pictures in your reader's mind in different ways. Try using **similes** to say that one thing is like another:

The moon was like a smiling face.

Some similes use the word as:

She was quick as an eel.

Metaphors say that one thing is another:

The candyfloss clouds drifted. *(See the poem on page 50.)*

Personification brings objects alive:

The trees waved their branches in the wind.

Make words work

When you write poems, choose powerful words. Read this sentence:

The cat went along the wall.

It would be more effective if it used powerful and precise language:

The Siamese limped along the red brick wall.

Try different types of poetry

In this dictionary you will find different types of poetry to inspire you. Have a go at writing your own poems based on the types below.

Haiku *(see pages 33, 45)*
These short poems come from Japan. They are usually three lines long and have a pattern of 5/7/5 syllables. You can also use your own syllable pattern.

Cinquain *(see pages 19, 59)*
These are like haiku. They have five lines and use a pattern of 2/4/6/8/2 syllables. You can also invent your own syllable pattern.

Limericks *(see page 68)*
These are often funny and usually have three long lines and two short ones. The rhyming pattern is aa/bb/a.

Riddles *(see page 28)*
These are fun to write. Try to give clues without giving the subject away.

Acrostics *(see page 91)*
These poems spell out a word in letters hidden somewhere within the lines. You read acrostics downwards.

Calligrams *(see pages 54-55)*
These are written so that the shape of the words reflect the meaning. On page 54 the letters of the words 'rolling pin' form the shape of a rolling pin.

Rhyming couplets *(see page 71)*
These are two lines which rhyme. You can invent other rhyming patterns, as in the poem on page 83, which uses the pattern aa/bb/a.

Word plays *(see pages 41, 93)*
Some poems play with words by taking them literally.

Rhyming games

Pass the rhyme
This is a quick game you can play anywhere. The first player says a word and the next has to say a rhyming word. The rhyming sound is passed on until no-one can think of another rhyming word.

Place names
This is a good game for journeys. Try finding rhymes for place names, or people's names, for example:

I felt loud
in Stroud,
picked my teeth
in Moncrieff...

Copycat
Think of a well-known nursery rhyme or song and copy it, changing some of the words. Look at the alternative version of Humpty Dumpty on page 14.

a

baa	aha	ha ha	papa
ha	gaga	hoo-ha	chihuahua
ma	grandma	hoopla	Panama
pa	grandpa	mama	tra-la-la

ar

bar	tar	crowbar	caviar
car	tsar	guitar	handlebar
far	afar	radar	jaguar
jar	ajar	sitar	movie star
scar	all-star	so far	near and far
spar	bazaar	towbar	superstar
star	crossbar	cable car	TV star

are

are

ab

blab	drab	jab	slab
cab	fab	lab	stab
crab	flab	nab	kebab
dab	grab	scab	minicab

abble

babble	dabble	gabble	scrabble

abby

crabby	flabby	shabby	tabby

able

able	times table
cable	timetable
fable	turntable
sable	unable
stable	unstable
table	willing and able

abel

label

Carla the baby-faced chihuahua chased
Abby the dirty-faced tabby ...

ace

ace	airspace	retrace	hiding place
brace	birthplace	sack race	human race
face	deface	shoelace	in your face
grace	disgrace	snail's pace	outer space
lace	embrace	unlace	out of place
pace	fireplace	workspace	pride of place
place	horse race	baby face	relay race
race	lose face	commonplace	saving grace
space	misplace	double-space	blue in the face
trace	replace	face to face	obstacle race

ase

base	bookcase	suitcase	pillowcase
case	nutcase	database	wild goose
chase	staircase	just in case	chase

aced

braced	spaced	fast-paced	straitlaced
faced	traced	misplaced	two-faced
graced	barefaced	outpaced	unlaced
laced	defaced	red-faced	angel-faced
paced	disgraced	replaced	baby-faced
placed	displaced	retraced	dirty-faced
raced	embraced	shamefaced	interlaced

aist

waist

aste

haste	taste	bad taste	toothpaste
paste	waste	good taste	cut and paste

ack

back	snack	horseback	unpack
black	stack	humpback	wisecrack
crack	thwack	hunchback	answer back
hack	track	icepack	back to back
jack	whack	laid back	heart attack
knack	attack	outback	jumping jack
lack	backpack	racetrack	lumberjack
pack	backtrack	ransack	paperback
quack	bareback	rucksack	piggyback
rack	drawback	setback	single track
sack	flapjack	sidetrack	stickleback
shack	flashback	soundtrack	Union Jack
slack	haystack	switchback	clackity-clack
smack	hijack	tailback	pat on the back

ac

mac	tarmac	cul-de-sac	zodiac
sac	bric-a-brac	maniac	insomniac

ak

yak	kayak	anorak	yakkity-yak

aque

plaque

ackle

cackle	tackle
crackle	ramshackle
shackle	

ackal

jackal

Rain smacks
attacks
ramshackle
back streets.
Lightning crackles,
cracks
the glistening back
of the tarmac
night.

acks

cracks	shacks	attacks	rucksacks
jacks	smacks	backpacks	setbacks
lacks	snacks	backtracks	sidetracks
packs	stacks	flapjacks	soundtracks
quacks	thwacks	haystacks	switchbacks
racks	tracks	hijacks	unpacks
sacks	whacks	ransacks	railway tracks

aks

yaks	kayaks	anoraks

ax

fax	tax	earwax	income tax
lax	wax	relax	to the max
max	beeswax	thorax	
sax	climax	candle wax	

axe

axe	pickaxe	poleaxe	battle-axe

act

act	attract	extract	overact
fact	compact	impact	riot act
pact	contract	react	matter of fact
tact	distract	subtract	overreact
abstract	exact	artefact	put on an act

acked

backed	sacked	whacked	jam-packed
blacked	slacked	attacked	ransacked
cracked	smacked	backpacked	sidetracked
hacked	snacked	backtracked	unpacked
lacked	stacked	hijacked	vacuum-packed
packed	thwacked	humpbacked	
quacked	tracked	hunchbacked	

ad

bad	lad	launch pad	mum and dad
clad	mad	nomad	not all bad
dad	pad	not bad	shoulder pad
fad	sad	Sinbad	Trinidad
glad	granddad	too bad	stark raving
had	kneepad	ironclad	mad

add

add

ade

blade	trade	invade	centigrade
fade	wade	lampshade	escapade
glade	arcade	parade	fire brigade
grade	decade	persuade	lemonade
jade	evade	sunshade	marmalade
made	grenade	unmade	orangeade
shade	handmade	barricade	ready-made
spade	homemade	cavalcade	shoulder blade

aid

braid	raid	first aid	well-paid
laid	staid	mermaid	hearing aid
maid	afraid	repaid	overpaid
paid	bridesmaid	unpaid	underpaid

ayed

brayed	sprayed	arrayed	displayed
frayed	stayed	betrayed	portrayed
played	strayed	decayed	replayed
prayed	swayed	delayed	x-rayed

ede

suede

eighed

neighed	sleighed	weighed	outweighed

eyed

obeyed	preyed	surveyed	disobeyed

12

aft

craft	raft	crankshaft	witchcraft
daft	shaft	life raft	fore and aft
graft	aircraft	spacecraft	hovercraft

aughed

laughed

aught

draught

ag

bag	rag	chinwag	teabag
brag	sag	handbag	windbag
crag	snag	jet lag	zigzag
drag	stag	name tag	doggy bag
flag	swag	postbag	hoist the flag
gag	tag	price tag	pack your bag
hag	wag	punchbag	saddlebag
lag	air bag	ratbag	scallywag
nag	beanbag	sandbag	sleeping bag

age

age	birdcage	old age	teenage
cage	Bronze Age	outrage	upstage
page	enrage	rampage	web page
rage	front page	rib cage	Iron Age
stage	Ice Age	space age	under age
wage	offstage	Stone Age	
backstage			

Love poem

I'll be your –
handmade hearing aid,
homemade sunshade,
underpaid barricade.

Humpty Dumpty
Sat on a nail.
Humpty Dumpty
Turned quite pale.

Humpty Dumpty
Swallowed a snail.
Humpty Dumpty
Felt quite frail.

ale

ale	sale	female	fairytale
bale	scale	for sale	garage sale
dale	stale	impale	ginger ale
gale	tale	inhale	killer whale
male	whale	telltale	nightingale
pale	exhale	car boot sale	old wives' tale

ail

ail	pail	airmail	toenail
bail	quail	blackmail	fingernail
fail	rail	chainmail	Holy Grail
frail	sail	detail	monorail
hail	snail	e-mail	nature trail
jail	tail	fan mail	ponytail
mail	trail	pigtail	tooth and nail
nail	wail	thumbnail	without fail

air			
air	pair	funfair	unfair
chair	stair	highchair	wheelchair
fair	armchair	mid-air	off the air
flair	au pair	pushchair	on the air
hair	despair	repair	rocking chair
lair	éclair	thin air	walk on air

aire			
billionaire	millionaire	solitaire	

are			
bare	hare	square	fanfare
blare	mare	stare	hardware
care	rare	aware	nightmare
dare	scare	beware	prepare
fare	share	bus fare	set square
flare	snare	compare	software
glare	spare	declare	threadbare

ear			
bear	tear	nightwear	polar bear
pear	wear	sportswear	teddy bear
swear	footwear	grizzly bear	underwear

eir			
heir	their		

ere			
there	nowhere	anywhere	then and there
where	somewhere	everywhere	neither here nor
elsewhere	so there!	here and there	there

Complete the rhyme

As I was going up the stairs
I met a man with seven bears
Each ..... had six .....
Each ..... had five .....

15

airy

airy	fairy	tooth fairy	sugar plum fairy
dairy	hairy	airy-fairy	

airie
prairie

ary
scary
vary
wary
canary
contrary
unwary

ake

bake	shake	handbrake	Christmas cake
brake	snake	handshake	double take
cake	stake	keepsake	give and take
drake	take	milkshake	overtake
fake	wake	mistake	pat-a-cake
flake	awake	namesake	piece of cake
lake	cheesecake	oatcake	rattlesnake
make	earthquake	pancake	undertake
quake	fishcake	snowflake	wide-awake
rake	fruitcake	teacake	for goodness
sake	grass snake	birthday cake	sake

ache

ache	earache	heartache	bellyache
backache	headache	toothache	stomach ache

aque
opaque

eak

break	firebreak	rumpsteak	take a break
steak	heartbreak	tea break	coffee break
beefsteak	jailbreak	windbreak	give me a break
daybreak	outbreak	make or break	

all

all	birdcall	pinball	crystal ball
ball	bookstall	pitfall	free-for-all
call	downfall	play ball	know-it-all
fall	eyeball	rainfall	off-the-wall
hall	fireball	recall	on the ball
pall	football	snowball	overall
small	freefall	snowfall	shopping mall
squall	meatball	town hall	up the wall
stall	netball	windfall	volleyball
tall	nightfall	all in all	wall-to-wall
wall	oddball	basketball	waterfall
baseball	phone call	cannonball	fly on the wall

aul

haul	maul	caterwaul	overhaul

awl

bawl	crawl	scrawl	sprawl
brawl	drawl	shawl	trawl

alley

alley	galley	valley	blind alley

ally

pally	rally	tally	dilly-dally

am

am	pram	tram	diagram
clam	ram	wham	hologram
cram	scam	yam	in a jam
dam	scram	exam	kilogram
gram	sham	program	milligram
ham	slam	wigwam	traffic jam
jam	swam	anagram	battering ram

amb

lamb	door jamb

ame

blame	game	tame	surname
came	lame	ball game	claim to fame
fame	name	became	crying shame
flame	same	door frame	overcame
frame	shame	nickname	window frame

aim

aim	maim	exclaim	reclaim
claim	acclaim	proclaim	take aim

amp

camp	cramp	ramp	tramp
champ	damp	scamp	foglamp
clamp	lamp	stamp	postage stamp

amper

camper	hamper	scamper	picnic hamper
damper	pamper	tamper	

an

ban	plan	conman	frying pan
bran	ran	deadpan	handyman
can	scan	dustpan	highwayman
clan	span	Japan	man-to-man
fan	tan	kaftan	marzipan
flan	than	lifespan	Peter Pan
gran	van	marked man	right-hand man
man	began	sandman	spick and span
nan	caveman	suntan	catamaran
pan		time span	flash in the pan
		wingspan	orang-utan
		also-ran	removal van
		caravan	deliveryman

my gran is a fan of the orang-utan

-ance to -and

ance

chance	stance	entrance	tap dance
dance	trance	fat chance	fighting chance
France	advance	folk dance	half a chance
glance	barn dance	freelance	not a chance
lance	break dance	last chance	song and dance
prance	by chance	rain dance	take a chance

ants

chants	plants	enchants	pot plants
grants	slants	house plants	transplants

and

and	by hand	sweatband	overland
band	crash-land	wasteland	promised land
brand	dreamland	waveband	rubber band
gland	expand	withstand	secondhand
grand	forehand	beforehand	sleight of hand
hand	freehand	contraband	underhand
land	grandstand	fairyland	understand
sand	grassland	hand in hand	wonderland
stand	handstand	helping hand	cloud-cuckoo
strand	headstand	lend a hand	land
armband	offhand	no man's land	misunderstand
backhand	old hand	one man band	never-never
bandstand	quicksand	out of hand	land

anned

banned	fanned	planned	spanned
canned	manned	scanned	tanned

We scanned –
Empty shoreline,
Where oystercatchers stand –
Black and white wings flick; thin red beaks
Sift sand.

ane			
bane	mane	vane	aeroplane
cane	pane	wane	sugar cane
crane	plane	humane	weathervane
lane	sane	insane	windowpane

ain			
brain	plain	train	food chain
chain	rain	vain	remain
drain	Spain	again	tearstain
grain	sprain	complain	acid rain
main	stain	contain	down the drain
pain	strain	explain	scatterbrain

ein			
rein	vein	chow mein	

eign			
reign			

ang			
bang	hang	sang	twang
clang	pang	slang	chain gang
fang	prang	sprang	boomerang
gang	rang	tang	overhang

ingue			
meringue			

angle			
angle	mangle	strangle	rectangle
bangle	spangle	tangle	triangle
dangle		wrangle	untangle
jangle		quadrangle	jingle-jangle

Never let –
Your braces dangle –
When you're standing –
By a mangle!

ank

bank	frank	stank	point-blank
blank	lank	swank	sandbank
clank	plank	tank	bottle bank
crank	prank	thank	break the bank
dank	sank	yank	draw a blank
drank	shrank	fish tank	savings bank
flank	spank	gangplank	walk the plank

ant

ant	pant	rant	scant

antic

antic	Atlantic	pedantic	transatlantic
frantic	gigantic	romantic	unromantic

ap

bap	sap	cat flap	recap
cap	scrap	hubcap	suntrap
chap	slap	icecap	unwrap
clap	snap	kidnap	watchstrap
flap	strap	kneecap	baseball cap
gap	tap	last lap	booby trap
lap	trap	man trap	handicap
map	wrap	mishap	overlap
nap	yap	mousetrap	thinking cap
rap	zap	nightcap	thunderclap

ape

ape	escape
cape	landscape
drape	red tape
gape	seascape
grape	shipshape
nape	bow and scrape
scrape	fire escape
shape	out of shape
tape	narrow escape
agape	videotape

an ape
in a cape

arch

arch	March	starch	quick march
march	parch	frogmarch	on the march

ard

card	yard	graveyard	scorecard
guard	bombard	lifeguard	scrapyard
hard	coastguard	mallard	bodyguard
lard	farmyard	mudguard	credit card
shard	fireguard	postcard	leotard

arred

barred	marred	sparred	tarred
charred	scarred	starred	ill-starred

arf

scarf	headscarf

affe

giraffe

alf

calf	behalf	better half
half	other half	half and half

aph

graph	autograph	paragraph	photograph

augh

laugh	last laugh	belly laugh	hollow laugh

ark

ark	earmark	leap in the dark
bark	embark	safari park
dark	landmark	
hark	postmark	
lark	remark	
mark	skylark	
park	theme park	
shark	double-park	
spark	Noah's ark	
aardvark	question mark	
bookmark	keep in the dark	

DO NOT FEED THE SHARK

Keep calm –
The fire alarm
is a modern-day lucky charm

arm

arm	harm	arm-in-arm	lucky charm
charm	alarm	false alarm	overarm
farm	disarm	fire alarm	underarm

alm

calm	palm	psalm	qualm

art

art	tart	go-kart	upstart
cart	apart	head start	fall apart
dart	depart	jump-start	martial art
part	dustcart	kick-start	poles apart
smart	false start	outsmart	work of art
start	flow chart	Pop art	state-of-the-art

eart

heart	sweetheart	cross your heart	heavy heart
lose heart	take heart	have a heart	learn by heart

ash

ash	gash	smash	newsflash
bash	gnash	splash	slapdash
brash	hash	stash	whiplash
cash	lash	thrash	balderdash
clash	mash	trash	nappy rash
crash	rash	backlash	
dash	sash	eyelash	
flash	slash	gatecrash	

ask

ask	cask	mask	unmask
bask	flask	task	vacuum flask

asp

clasp	gasp	grasp	rasp

23

a -ass to -atch

ass

brass	pass	spyglass	smooth as glass
class	bypass	surpass	underpass
glass	first class	bold as brass	magnifying
grass	outclass	second class	glass

ast

blast	past	downcast	outlast
cast	vast	forecast	all-star cast
fast	aghast	full blast	at long last
last	at last	half-mast	first and last
mast	contrast	outcast	overcast

assed

classed	grassed	passed	surpassed

at

at	spat	old hat	just like that
bat	splat	place mat	pit-a-pat
brat	that	sunhat	puppy fat
cat	vat	tomcat	pussycat
chat	chitchat	top hat	scaredy cat
fat	combat	wildcat	smell a rat
flat	cowpat	wombat	tabby cat
gnat	dingbat	acrobat	this and that
hat	doormat	alley cat	tit for tat
mat	fall flat	babysat	ziggurat
pat	fat cat	copycat	aristocrat
rat	hardhat	cowboy hat	blind as a bat
sat	like that	habitat	rat-a-tat-tat

atch

catch	snatch	boxing match	shooting match
hatch	thatch	cabbage patch	slanging match
latch	crosspatch	elbow patch	tennis match
match	knee patch	football match	game, set and
patch	mismatch	met his match	match
scratch	unlatch	mix and match	

ach

attach	detach

ate

ate	frustrate	detonate	roller skate
crate	ice skate	duplicate	second-rate
date	irate	educate	sell-by date
fate	migrate	estimate	separate
gate	playmate	excavate	up to date
grate	primate	fascinate	vaccinate
hate	rotate	germinate	abbreviate
late	schoolmate	hesitate	accelerate
mate	shipmate	hibernate	appreciate
plate	stalemate	illustrate	assassinate
rate	third-rate	imitate	at any rate
skate	translate	incubate	communicate
state	update	indicate	cooperate
blind date	vibrate	insulate	deliberate
cheapskate	calculate	irritate	evaporate
checkmate	celebrate	make a date	exaggerate
create	complicate	meditate	exasperate
cut-rate	concentrate	number plate	interrogate
debate	confiscate	operate	investigate
estate	decorate	out of date	refrigerate
first-rate	demonstrate	overate	reverberate

aight
straight

ait
bait | wait | await | portrait

eight
eight	lightweight	overweight	figure of eight
freight	featherweight	paperweight	
weight	heavyweight	underweight	

ete
fête

Is a lightweight heavyweight
The same as a featherweight?

25

'Waiter, waiter, there's an alligator
With a calculator in my soup!'
'That adds up!' snapped the waiter.

ator

creator	spectator	escalator	operator
dictator	translator	illustrator	radiator
equator	alligator	incubator	simulator
narrator	calculator	navigator	ventilator

aiter

waiter

aitor

traitor

ater

| cater | grater | skater | see you later |
| crater | later | roller skater | sooner or later |

atter

batter	matter	splatter	mad as a hatter
chatter	natter	bespatter	mind over
clatter	patter	grey matter	matter
fatter	platter	pitter-patter	no laughing
flatter	scatter	what's the	matter
latter	shatter	matter?	

attle

| battle | cattle | rattle | tittle-tattle |

atty

| batty | chatty | patty | scatty |
| catty | natty | ratty | tatty |

ave

brave	pave	wave	shockwave
cave	rave	behave	microwave
crave	save	brainwave	misbehave
gave	shave	forgave	rant and rave
grave	slave	heatwave	tidal wave

ay

bay	way	Monday	break away
bray	archway	no way	break of day
clay	away	okay	by the way
day	betray	one-way	castaway
fray	birthday	pathway	holiday
hay	child's play	railway	market day
lay	decay	runway	Milky Way
may	delay	some day	motorway
pay	doorway	subway	night and day
play	essay	Sunday	runaway
pray	fair play	Thursday	Saturday
ray	Friday	Tuesday	stowaway
say	gangway	today	straightaway
spray	halfway	Wednesday	takeaway
stay	highway	weekday	wedding day
stray	hooray	x-ray	yesterday
sway	horseplay	alleyway	day after day
tray	midday	anyway	red-letter day

é

café	pâté	fiancé	fiancée

eigh

neigh	sleigh	weigh	bobsleigh

et

ballet	bouquet	chalet	sachet
beret	buffet	duvet	ricochet

ey

grey	prey	obey	disobey
hey	they	survey	

a -aze

aze			
blaze	gaze	laze	amaze
craze	glaze	maze	stargaze
daze	graze	raze	trailblaze
faze	haze	ablaze	stony gaze

aise			
praise	raise	mayonnaise	

ase			
phase	phrase	erase	rephrase

ays			
bays	stays	essays	x-rays
brays	strays	pathways	alleyways
days	sways	railways	castaways
frays	trays	runways	gamma rays
lays	ways	school days	holidays
pays	always	sideways	market days
plays	betrays	some days	nowadays
prays	birthdays	subways	runaways
rays	delays	Sundays	stowaways
sprays	doorways	weekdays	good old days

Guess the riddles

Tasty date
Once a year
   I come round
adding another candle
  to the icing
  on your cake ...

Skyline smoker
Sitting
   like a hat.
Smoking
   like a pipe ...

answers: birthdays chimney

e	be	me	we	excuse me
	he	she	posse	recipe

ea	flea	sea	deep-sea	sweet pea
	pea	tea	high tea	China Sea
	plea	chickpea	North Sea	undersea

ee	bee	wee	settee	guarantee
	fee	agree	sightsee	honeybee
	flee	carefree	tee-hee	jamboree
	free	coffee	teepee	jubilee
	glee	degree	toffee	oversee
	knee	marquee	yippee	pedigree
	see	oak tree	bumblebee	referee
	spree	pine tree	busy bee	refugee
	tee	queen bee	chimpanzee	shopping spree
	three	rupee	Christmas tree	family tree
	tree	set free	disagree	fiddle-de-dee

ey	key	donkey	latchkey	monkey
	chimney	honey	money	valley

i	ski	graffiti	waterski	macaroni

ie	genie	pixie	zombie	walkie-talkie

uay	quay

Rhyming abbreviations
ending in -e sounds

AD   CFC IT   RIP
BC   DVD PC   RSVP
CD   ID   PE   VIP

I C
U C
we both C
the DVD!

Have U
N E
games
for the PC?

eaf	leaf	sheaf	cloverleaf	overleaf

eef	beef	reef	coral reef	roast beef

ief	brief	grief	belief	relief
	chief	thief	big chief	handkerchief

if	motif

eal	deal	seal	big deal	reveal
	heal	squeal	conceal	unreal
	meal	steal	ideal	wholemeal
	peal	zeal	oatmeal	
	real	appeal	ordeal	

eel	eel	keel	reel	cartwheel
	feel	kneel	steel	freewheel
	heel	peel	wheel	high heel

ile	imbecile	snowmobile	automobile	

eam	beam	steam	ice cream	sunbeam
	cream	stream	mainstream	suncream
	dream	team	moonbeam	upstream
	gleam	bloodstream	off beam	whipped cream
	scream	daydream	pipe dream	in a dream
	seam	downstream	slipstream	let off steam

eem	seem	teem	redeem	self-esteem

eme	scheme	theme	extreme	supreme

Davy Crockett
famous musketeer,
Had three ears –
A left ear, a right ear
And a wild frontier!

ear				
clear	rear	hear! hear!	in the clear
dear	shear	no fear	loud and clear
ear	smear	unclear	never fear
fear	spear	pierced ear	overhear
gear	tear	crystal clear	reappear
hear	all clear	disappear	
near	appear	far and near	

eer				
beer	peer	career	mountaineer
cheer	sheer	reindeer	musketeer
deer	sneer	buccaneer	pioneer
jeer	steer	engineer	puppeteer
leer	veer	ginger beer	volunteer

ere				
here	revere	atmosphere	insincere
mere	severe	biosphere	persevere
sphere	sincere	hemisphere	stratosphere

ier				
pier	cashier	cavalier	gondolier
tier	frontier	chandelier	

ir				
souvenir				

e -east to -eat

east

beast	least	beanfeast	southeast
east	yeast	northeast	last but not
feast	at least	not least	least

eased

ceased	greased	deceased	increased
creased	leased	decreased	released

iced

policed

ieced

pieced

easy

easy	queasy	uneasy	easy-peasy

eezy

breezy	sneezy	wheezy	lemon squeezy

eat

beat	neat	backseat	hot seat
bleat	peat	deadbeat	mincemeat
cheat	pleat	dead heat	repeat
eat	seat	defeat	retreat
feat	teat	drumbeat	overheat
heat	treat	front seat	overeat
meat	wheat	heartbeat	trick or treat

eet

feet	street	discreet	find your feet
fleet	sweet	groundsheet	itchy feet
greet	tweet	flat feet	parakeet
meet	backstreet	worksheet	short and sweet
sheet	big feet	bittersweet	two left feet
sleet	cold feet	drag your feet	

ete

athlete
compete
complete
delete

eater	beater	heater	anteater	fire eater
	eater	neater	eggbeater	two-seater

eetah	cheetah			

eeter	sweeter	teeter		

eter	meter	parking meter		

etre	metre	centimetre	kilometre	millimetre

itre	litre	centilitre	millilitre	

eck	beck	peck	spot-check	risk your neck
	check	speck	bottleneck	smart aleck
	deck	wreck	double check	pain in the neck
	fleck	breakneck	neck and neck	up to your
	neck	shipwreck	polo neck	neck

ech	Czech	high-tech		

ek	trek	pony trek		

eque	cheque	blank cheque	pay cheque	discotheque

Smart Aleck, clever clogs,
Ran a spot-check on his dogs.
Found with ease

– forty fleas!

e -ecks to -ect

ecks				
	checks	pecks	shipwrecks	double checks
	decks	specks	spot-checks	polo necks
	flecks	wrecks	bottlenecks	up to your necks
	necks	henpecks	clear the decks	

ex				
	flex	vex	index	perplex

ect				
	sect	infect	protect	disrespect
	collect	inject	reflect	incorrect
	connect	insect	reject	self-respect
	correct	inspect	respect	sound effect
	detect	neglect	select	cause and
	direct	object	subject	effect
	effect	perfect	suspect	to no effect
	eject	prefect	dialect	to good effect
	expect	project	disconnect	to take effect

ecked				
	checked	pecked	henpecked	spot-checked
	flecked	wrecked	shipwrecked	double checked

My uncle Rex
gets henpecked.

His wife says
this is to good effect.

If spot-checked
you can see where the beaks
have left their mark ...

My brother said
he'd lost his head –
we found it in
the garden shed!

ed

bed	sled	moped	flowerbed
bled	sped	sickbed	double bed
bred	wed	spoonfed	garden shed
fed	airbed	toolshed	infrared
fled	bloodshed	well-fed	newlywed
led	bobsled	woodshed	overfed
red	bunk bed	born and bred	quadruped
shed	deathbed	bottle fed	single bed
shred	misled	feather bed	underfed

aid

said

ead

bread	behead	shortbread	overhead
dead	big head	skinhead	scratch your
dread	blackhead	unthread	head
head	crispbread	well-read	shake your
lead	drop dead	widespread	head
read	egghead	arrowhead	sleepyhead
spread	forehead	figurehead	straight ahead
stead	hothead	gingerbread	full speed
thread	instead	go-ahead	ahead
tread	outspread	hang your head	go to his head
ahead	pinhead	keep your head	off with her
bedspread	redhead	left for dead	head
bedstead	Roundhead	lose your head	over his head

edge

dredge	ledge	wedge	razor's edge
edge	pledge	knife edge	
hedge	sledge	on edge	

e -eece to -eed

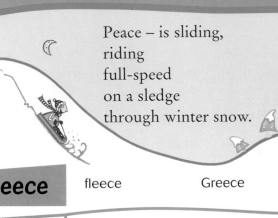

Peace – is sliding,
riding
full-speed
on a sledge
through winter snow.

Peace – is a seed
greedy to grow
as you gather speed
lip-reading
the winter wind.

eece	fleece	Greece		

eace	peace	world peace		

ease	cease	grease	decrease	release
	crease	lease	increase	elbow grease

ice	police	secret police		

iece	niece	hairpiece	mantelpiece	piece by piece
	piece	timepiece	masterpiece	all in one piece

eed	bleed	reed	duckweed	spoon-feed
	breed	seed	exceed	succeed
	creed	speed	full speed	take heed
	deed	steed	indeed	disagreed
	feed	tweed	knock-kneed	gather speed
	freed	weed	misdeed	guaranteed
	greed	agreed	nosebleed	hour of need
	heed	airspeed	proceed	refereed
	need	birdseed	seaweed	waterweed

ead	bead	plead	mislead	reread
	knead	read	misread	sight-read
	lead	lip-read	proofread	speed-read

ede	swede	stampede	centipede	millipede

eek

cheek	leek	seek	cheek-to-cheek
creek	meek	sleek	hide-and-seek
eek!	peek	week	tongue-in-cheek
Greek	reek	midweek	

eak

beak	freak	sneak	tweak
bleak	leak	speak	weak
creak	peak	squeak	so to speak

iek

shriek

ique

clique	boutique	oblique	unique
antique	mystique	technique	fit of pique

een

been	teen	pea-green	evergreen
green	between	sea-green	fairy queen
keen	canteen	sixteen	go-between
preen	eighteen	smokescreen	Hallowe'en
queen	fifteen	sunscreen	movie screen
screen	foreseen	thirteen	multi-screen
seen	fourteen	umpteen	seventeen
sheen	has-been	unseen	sweet sixteen
spleen	nineteen	windscreen	unforeseen

ean

bean	lean	dry-clean	lean and mean
clean	mean	green bean	runner bean
glean	wean	jelly bean	squeaky clean

ene

gene	scene	hygiene	serene

ine

chlorine	routine	limousine	slot machine
cuisine	sardine	magazine	submarine
machine	vaccine	margarine	tambourine
marine	clementine	nectarine	tangerine
ravine	guillotine	quarantine	trampoline

eep

beep	keep	sweep	skin-deep
bleep	peep	weep	upkeep
cheep	seep	asleep	ankle-deep
creep	sheep	Bo-Peep	beauty sleep
deep	sleep	black sheep	chimney sweep
jeep	steep	knee-deep	oversleep

eap

cheap	heap	leap	reap

ees

bees	agrees	bumblebees	jamborees
fees	decrees	busy bees	oversees
flees	degrees	chimpanzees	pedigrees
frees	marquees	Christmas trees	referees
knees	rupees	disagrees	refugees
sees	sightsees	dungarees	shopping
sprees	teepees	guarantees	sprees
trees	toffees	honeybees	the bees' knees

eas

fleas	pleas	chickpeas	sweet peas
peas	seas	high seas	overseas

ease

ease	please	tease	disease

eese

cheese	big cheese	say cheese	soft cheese

eize

seize

ese

these	Chinese	Japanese	Pekinese

eys

keys	donkeys
chimneys	monkeys

eze

breeze	sneeze	wheeze	unfreeze
freeze	squeeze	trapeze	antifreeze

eg	beg	keg	bad egg	chicken-and-
	dreg	leg	nutmeg	egg
	egg	peg	off the peg	an arm and a leg

ell	bell	swell	farewell	magic spell
	cell	tell	misspell	prison cell
	dwell	well	nutshell	very well
	fell	yell	oil well	wishing well
	hell	bluebell	retell	alive and well
	quell	bombshell	seashell	clear as a bell
	sell	cowbell	unwell	not very well
	shell	doorbell	cockleshell	saved by the
	smell	dumbbell	dinner bell	bell
	spell	eggshell	just as well	sound as a bell

el	gel	hotel	propel	carousel
	excel	lapel	rebel	citadel
	expel	motel	caramel	parallel

| **ello** | cello | hello | | |

| **ellow** | bellow | fellow | mellow | yellow |

Bellow 'hello' to the mellow yellow fellow as he plays on his cello.

| **elp** | help | kelp | whelp | yelp |

e -elt to -ench

elt
belt	felt	pelt	at full pelt
Celt	knelt	heartfelt	below the belt
dwelt	melt	seatbelt	under your belt

em
gem	stem	mayhem	Bethlehem
hem	them	modem	

en
den	pen	yen	citizen
fen	ten	amen	felt-tip pen
glen	then	Big Ben	fountain pen
hen	when	pigpen	lion's den
men	wren	playpen	mother hen

The job of Big Ben,
famous London citizen,
Is to tell you when ...

ence
fence	defence	pretence	sit on the fence
pence	offence	self-defence	

ense
dense	expense	incense	sixth sense
sense	good sense	make sense	suspense
tense	immense	nonsense	common sense

ench
bench	drench	quench	trench
clench	French	stench	wrench

I tend to drive
my girlfriend
round the bend –
but she catches a bus back!

end

bend	attend	extend	wits' end
blend	backbend	girlfriend	apprehend
end	bad end	intend	bitter end
friend	befriend	Land's End	end to end
lend	best friend	offend	on the mend
mend	boyfriend	pen friend	overspend
send	dead end	pretend	recommend
spend	deep end	sharp end	sticky end
tend	defend	suspend	around the
trend	depend	unbend	bend
ascend	descend	upend	at a loose end

ender

blender	lender	tender	offender
fender	sender	big spender	surrender
gender	slender	defender	weekender

ent

bent	went	lament	compliment
cent	ascent	per cent	discontent
dent	cement	present	heaven sent
lent	consent	prevent	main event
rent	content	relent	ornament
scent	descent	resent	overspent
sent	event	torment	represent
spent	for rent	well-spent	experiment
tent	fragment	big event	happy event
vent	invent	came and went	in any event

eant

leant	meant

ept			
crept	swept	except	windswept
kept	wept	inept	intercept
slept	accept	rainswept	overslept

epped		
stepped	sidestepped	overstepped

erry			
berry	merry	gooseberry	strawberry
cherry	blackberry	make merry	elderberry
ferry	blueberry	raspberry	

ery
very

ury
bury

esh			
flesh	mesh	afresh	refresh
fresh	thresh	gooseflesh	in the flesh

ess			
bless	access	helpless	success
chess	address	impress	sundress
cress	caress	kindness	undress
dress	confess	lifeless	unless
guess	depress	mattress	fancy dress
less	digress	nightdress	loneliness
mess	distress	oppress	more or less
press	duress	possess	new address
stress	excess	princess	nonetheless
tress	express	progress	second-guess
abcess	headdress	repress	watercress

es
yes

est

best	vest	head-rest	all the best
chest	west	infest	do your best
crest	zest	invest	driving test
guest	arrest	next best	hornet's nest
jest	bequest	northwest	last request
lest	conquest	protest	level best
nest	contest	request	past its best
pest	crow's nest	southwest	treasure chest
quest	detest	suggest	bulletproof vest
rest	digest	unrest	under arrest
test	foot-rest	Wild West	

east

breast	abreast	red-breast

essed

blessed	stressed	digressed	possessed
dressed	addressed	distressed	progressed
guessed	caressed	expressed	undressed
messed	confessed	impressed	overdressed
pressed	depressed	obsessed	unimpressed

In my mind's treasure chest –
Is a hornet's nest of ideas, restlessly buzzing;
Is the contest between the unicorn and the lion,
observed by an unimpressed robin red-breast;
Is a nest of comfort, where the strangest guest rests,
a jester that I call 'Imagination'.

e -et to -eve

et

bet	wet	handset	Tibet
fret	yet	headset	upset
get	all set	jet set	alphabet
jet	dragnet	not yet	clarinet
met	duet	quartet	dripping wet
net	filmset	quick set	Internet
pet	fishnet	quintet	safety net
set	forget	regret	teacher's pet
vet	get set	sunset	

eat

sweat threat

ette

baguette	croquette	roulette	serviette
brunette	launderette	kitchenette	silhouette
cassette	omelette	maisonette	usherette
courgette	rosette	pirouette	

etch

fetch sketch stretch wretch

ettle

kettle mettle nettle settle

etal

metal petal rose petal heavy metal

eve

eve sleeve Christmas Eve

eave

heave leave weave

eive

deceive perceive receive

ieve

grieve	believe	reprieve	disbelieve
achieve	relieve	retrieve	make-believe

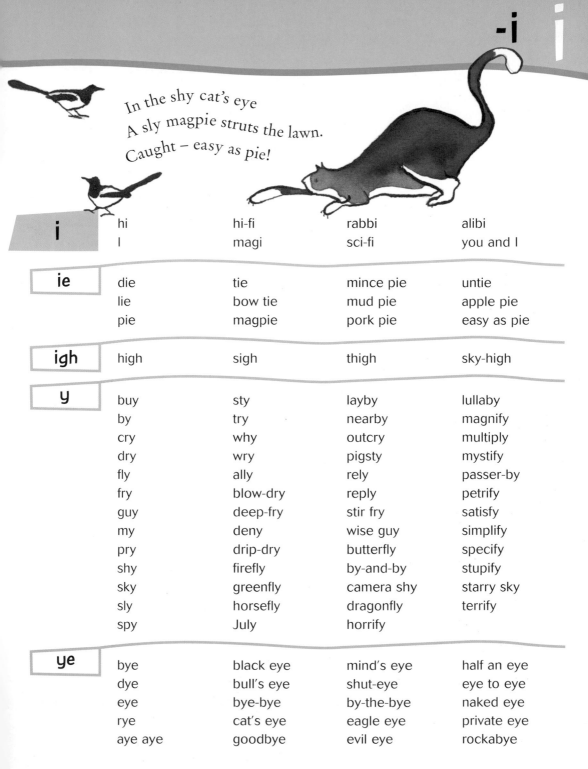

In the shy cat's eye
A sly magpie struts the lawn.
Caught – easy as pie!

| i | hi | hi-fi | rabbi | alibi |
| | I | magi | sci-fi | you and I |

ie	die	tie	mince pie	untie
	lie	bow tie	mud pie	apple pie
	pie	magpie	pork pie	easy as pie

| igh | high | sigh | thigh | sky-high |

y	buy	sty	layby	lullaby
	by	try	nearby	magnify
	cry	why	outcry	multiply
	dry	wry	pigsty	mystify
	fly	ally	rely	passer-by
	fry	blow-dry	reply	petrify
	guy	deep-fry	stir fry	satisfy
	my	deny	wise guy	simplify
	pry	drip-dry	butterfly	specify
	shy	firefly	by-and-by	stupify
	sky	greenfly	camera shy	starry sky
	sly	horsefly	dragonfly	terrify
	spy	July	horrify	

ye	bye	black eye	mind's eye	half an eye
	dye	bull's eye	shut-eye	eye to eye
	eye	bye-bye	by-the-bye	naked eye
	rye	cat's eye	eagle eye	private eye
	aye aye	goodbye	evil eye	rockabye

i -ib to -ick

ib	bib	crib	fib	rib

ibble	dribble	nibble	quibble	scribble

ice	dice	price	trice	half-price
	ice	rice	twice	think twice
	lice	slice	advice	break the ice
	mice	spice	black ice	once or twice
	nice	splice	cut-price	sacrifice

ise	concise	precise	paradise	fool's paradise

ick	brick	sick	drumstick	pinprick
	chick	slick	gimmick	seasick
	click	stick	hat trick	candlestick
	flick	thick	homesick	dirty trick
	kick	tick	lipstick	double quick
	lick	trick	matchstick	limerick
	pick	broomstick	nitpick	pogo stick
	quick	chopstick	non-stick	walking stick

ic	hic	tactic	mosaic	acrobatic
	attic	tragic	organic	automatic
	basic	bionic	Pacific	prehistoric
	comic	elastic	terrific	supersonic
	garlic	electric		
	hectic	fantastic		
	magic	historic		
	music	horrific		
	panic	lunatic		
	picnic	majestic		
	plastic	mechanic		
	public	metallic		

icks				
	bricks	picks	chopsticks	bag of tricks
	chicks	pricks	drumsticks	candlesticks
	clicks	sticks	for kicks	dirty tricks
	flicks	ticks	hand-picks	fiddlesticks
	kicks	tricks	gimmicks	pick-up-sticks
	licks	broomsticks	matchsticks	ton of bricks
	nicks	card tricks	pinpricks	walking sticks

ics				
	tics	comics	tropics	gymnastics
	antics	picnics	aerobics	hysterics

ix				
	fix	cake mix	quick fix	pick and mix
	mix	matrix	appendix	twenty-six
	six	phoenix	in a fix	sixty-six

id				
	bid	quid	forbid	timid
	did	rid	humid	valid
	grid	skid	liquid	vivid
	hid	slid	livid	whizz kid
	kid	squid	rapid	invalid
	lid	eyelid	rigid	pyramid

iddle			
	diddle	middle	fit as a fiddle
	fiddle	riddle	pig in the
	griddle	twiddle	middle

DIY nursery rhyme

Hey diddle diddle, one pig in the middle,
Two mice leapt over the sun,
The little cat purred to see such fun
And the dog flew away with the bun!

i -ide

ide			
bride	tide	high tide	seaside
glide	wide	hillside	worldwide
guide	aside	inside	alongside
hide	astride	joyride	countryside
pride	backside	landslide	far and wide
ride	bedside	low tide	pesticide
side	decide	offside	riverside
slide	divide	outside	side by side
stride	fireside	roadside	slip and slide

ied			
cried	spied	relied	multiplied
died	tied	replied	mystified
dried	tried	tongue-tied	petrified
fried	deep-fried	untied	satisfied
lied	denied	horrified	terrified

ighed			
sighed			

yed			
eyed	cock-eyed	pop-eyed	eagle-eyed
bright-eyed	cross-eyed	red-eyed	goggle-eyed

Listen

At the riverside
Listen to the tongue-tied reeds
Whisper in the wind.

At the seaside
listen to the slow *slip* and *slide*
of the restless tide.

At the roadside
Listen to the goggle-eyed drivers
Tied to the wheel.

At the fireside
Listen to the bright-eyed flame
name the hearth and heart.

idge

bridge	midge	squidge	footbridge
fridge	ridge	drawbridge	porridge

ies

cries	spies	French fries	dragonflies
dies	ties	magpies	horrifies
dries	tries	mince pies	lullabies
flies	blow-dries	mud pies	magnifies
fries	blue skies	pigsties	multiplies
lies	bow ties	pork pies	petrifies
pies	deep-fries	replies	starry skies
skies	fireflies	butterflies	terrifies

ighs

highs	sighs	thighs

ise

guise	advise	high-rise	unwise
prise	arise	likewise	advertise
rise	clockwise	sunrise	exercise
wise	disguise	surprise	televise

ize

prize	king-size	hypnotize	mobilize
size	life-size	idolize	realize
capsize	outsize	memorize	recognize
first prize	booby prize	mesmerize	apologize

ife

knife	jackknife	large as life	husband and
life	penknife	pocketknife	wife
wife	wildlife	true to life	not on your life

iff

biff	sniff	tiff	scared stiff
cliff	stiff	whiff	skewwhiff

if

if	as if	what if?

Snowdrift

Overnight
Snow drifts,
And leaves a gift of white.
Twigs wear judge's wigs.

Midnight moonlight
Invites the moon's soft lamplight.

Tonight, starlight speckles the dark.
The wind lifts soft drifts.

Streetlights take the limelight –
Write cold messages in the darkness.

Headlights blare –
A fox freezes, trapped in stage fright,
Takes swift goodnight flight for home.

ift			
drift	shift	adrift	shoplift
gift	sift	face lift	ski lift
lift	swift	makeshift	snowdrift
rift	thrift	night shift	spendthrift

iffed			
biffed	miffed	sniffed	whiffed

ig			
big	jig	twig	oil rig
dig	pig	wig	guinea pig
fig	sprig	bigwig	whirligig
gig	swig	earwig	

iggle			
giggle	niggle	wiggle	
jiggle	squiggle	wriggle	

ight

bright	all right	limelight	upright
fight	bullfight	midnight	candlelight
flight	daylight	moonlight	copyright
fright	delight	outright	day or night
height	eyesight	oversight	dead of night
knight	firelight	playwright	fly-by-night
light	fistfight	searchlight	out of sight
might	flashlight	skintight	overnight
night	floodlight	skylight	pillow fight
plight	forthright	spotlight	second-sight
right	fortnight	stage fright	see the light
sight	good night	starlight	watertight
slight	headlight	streetlight	opening night
tight	highlight	sunlight	out like a light
airtight	insight	tonight	sweetness and
all-night	lamplight	twilight	light

ite

bite	white	polite	black and white
kite	write	recite	dynamite
mite	fleabite	snake bite	parasite
quite	frostbite	unite	satellite
site	ignite	website	stalactite
spite	invite	ammonite	stalagmite
sprite	not quite	appetite	meteorite

yte

byte	megabyte

ike

bike	strike	hitchhike	hunger strike
hike	alike	lifelike	ladylike
like	childlike	snakelike	look-alike
pike	dislike	unlike	motorbike
spike	ghostlike	warlike	unalike

ild	child	mild	wild	godchild

iled	filed	piled	smiled	tiled

ile	file	vile	missile	worthwhile
	mile	while	mobile	crocodile
	Nile	agile	nail file	in a while
	pile	awhile	profile	run a mile
	smile	fragile	reptile	single file
	stile	hostile	turnstile	worth your
	tile	meanwhile	woodpile	while

ial	dial	phial	trial	sundial

isle	aisle	isle		

yle	style	freestyle	hairstyle	lifestyle

ill	bill	kill	till	refill
	brill	mill	trill	sawmill
	chill	pill	will	standstill
	dill	quill	anthill	treadmill
	drill	shrill	downhill	uphill
	fill	sill	fire drill	windmill
	frill	skill	goodwill	overfill
	gill	spill	ill will	overkill
	grill	still	molehill	underfill
	hill	swill	oil spill	windowsill
	ill	thrill	pigswill	over the hill

il	nil	fulfil	until	daffodil
	anvil	tranquil	vigil	

illy	chilly	hilly	silly-billy
	frilly	silly	willy-nilly

illi	chilli

ily	lily	readily	steadily
	merrily	Sicily	water lily

ilt	hilt	kilt	spilt	tilt
	jilt	lilt	stilt	wilt

uilt	built	guilt	quilt	well built

im	brim	prim	swim	minim
	dim	rim	trim	pilgrim
	grim	skim	whim	
	him	slim	denim	

imb	limb

ym	gym	antonym	pseudonym	synonym

ymn	hymn

Athletic poem
(say it quickly)

Tim met prim Kim at the gym.
Said Tim to Kim,
'How do you keep such slim limbs Kim?'
'I swim till I'm trim, Tim!' said Kim.

ime

chime	full-time	sometime	pantomime
crime	half-time	springtime	party time
dime	high time	teatime	summertime
grime	lifetime	anytime	suppertime
lime	meantime	behind time	wintertime
mime	night-time	dinnertime	all in good time
prime	on time	every time	many a time
slime	part-time	half the time	not before time
time	pastime	harvest time	one at a time
bedtime	peacetime	keep in time	time after time
big time	playtime	one more time	in the nick of
daytime	prime time	overtime	time

imb

climb

yme

rhyme	thyme	enzyme	nursery rhyme

in

bin	twin	javelin	within
chin	win	margin	double chin
fin	bearskin	muffin	drawing pin
grin	begin	penguin	hobgoblin
in	break-in	puffin	mandarin
kin	cabin	pumpkin	origin
pin	catkin	robin	rolling pin
shin	coffin	ruin	safety pin
sin	dolphin	satin	terrapin
skin	dustbin	sequin	thick and thin
spin	goblin	sheepskin	tigerskin
thin	gremlin	stand-in	violin
tin	hairpin	tailspin	vitamin

THIN ROLLING PIN

inch			
clinch	inch	winch	inch by inch
flinch	pinch	feel the pinch	pennypinch

ind			
bind	rind	snow-blind	lemon rind
blind	wind	unkind	mastermind
find	behind	unwind	never mind
grind	mankind	bear in mind	open mind
kind	remind	colourblind	peace of mind
mind	rewind	humankind	spring to mind

igned	
signed	

ined			
dined	pined	outlined	underlined
lined	whined	streamlined	undermined

ine			
brine	whine	grapevine	sunshine
dine	wine	guideline	touchline
fine	airline	headline	borderline
line	alpine	hotline	draw the line
mine	beeline	lifeline	first in line
nine	canine	moonshine	hold the line
pine	clothesline	outline	porcupine
shine	coastline	outshine	rain or shine
spine	cloud nine	pipeline	rise and shine
swine	combine	punchline	storyline
twine	divine	shoeshine	underline
vine	gold mine	skyline	valentine

ign			
sign	design	resign	stop sign

ing

bring	wring	fishing	stunning
cling	zing	hearing	whaling
fling	bee sting	living	writing
king	boring	nosering	amusing
ping	building	nothing	anything
ring	bullring	pudding	day-dreaming
sing	ceiling	racing	diamond ring
sling	changeling	railing	everything
spring	clothing	roaring	exciting
sting	cunning	running	freewheeling
string	doing	sitting	hair-raising
swing	duckling	skating	spine-chilling
thing	earring	something	surprising
wing	farming	spelling	

inge

binge	fringe	singe	twinge
cringe	hinge	tinge	syringe

ink

blink	link	stink	in a wink
brink	mink	think	let me think
chink	pink	wink	missing link
clink	rink	hoodwink	on the blink
drink	shrink	ice rink	pen and ink
ink	sink	rethink	skating rink
kink	slink	soft drink	tickled pink

inc

zinc

What does this picture poem say?

I   think   you   stink!

int

flint	skint	footprint	spearmint
glint	splint	misprint	thumbprint
hint	squint	newsprint	drop a hint
mint	tint	reprint	fingerprint
print	blueprint	skinflint	peppermint

ip

blip	quip	airstrip	comic strip
chip	rip	cowslip	fingertip
clip	ship	field trip	leadership
dip	sip	friendship	lose your grip
drip	skip	gossip	membership
flip	slip	hardship	microchip
grip	snip	non-slip	paperclip
hip	strip	sheep dip	pirate ship
kip	tip	spaceship	championship
lip	trip	tulip	citizenship
nip	whip	warship	premiership
pip	zip	battleship	silicon chip

ipe

gripe	swipe	hornpipe	windpipe
pipe	wipe	peace pipe	guttersnipe
ripe	bagpipe	pinstripe	overripe
stripe	drainpipe	unripe	underripe

ype

hype	type	prototype	stereotype

ire

dire	backfire	empire	perspire
fire	barbed wire	for hire	quagmire
hire	bonfire	gunfire	sapphire
spire	campfire	haywire	vampire
tire	catch fire	inspire	wildfire
wire	desire	on fire	forest fire

yre

tyre	flat tyre

-is to -ist

is	his	is	as is	
iz	quiz	showbiz		
izz	fizz	frizz	swizz	whizz

ish	dish	wish	punish	shellfish
	fish	brandish	rubbish	starfish
	squish	goldfish	selfish	vanish
	swish	perish	sheepish	jellyfish

isk	brisk	risk	hard disk	compact disk
	disk	whisk	asterisk	take a risk

iss	bliss	miss	dismiss	hit or miss
	kiss	amiss	near miss	give it a miss

ice	malice	practice	apprentice	precipice
	novice	service	cowardice	self-service
	office	accomplice	liquorice	secret service

is	this	Paris	trellis	emphasis
	axis	tennis	chrysalis	portcullis

ist	fist	mist	cellist	insist
	gist	twist	checklist	resist
	list	wrist	cyclist	tourist

issed	hissed	kissed	missed	dismissed

sSSS

it			
bit	slit	habit	visit
fit	spit	moonlit	babysit
flit	split	orbit	bit by bit
grit	twit	outfit	every bit
hit	wit	outwit	first-aid kit
it	admit	permit	inhabit
kit	armpit	rabbit	inherit
knit	bandit	smash hit	not a bit
lit	biscuit	summit	perfect fit
nit	bluetit	sunlit	prohibit
pit	circuit	that's it	throw a fit
quit	cockpit	tight fit	banana split
sit	culprit	tool kit	lickety-spit

et			
basket	fidget	nugget	rocket
bracelet	gadget	piglet	secret
bucket	helmet	pocket	ticket
carpet	jacket	puppet	triplet
cricket	magnet	racket	trumpet

Moonlit!
Stars are bracelets.
Dark inhabits the park.
Sudden scarlet splits the night sky.
Rocket!

i -itch to -iver

itch			
ditch	itch	stitch	witch
glitch	pitch	switch	bewitch
hitch	snitch	twitch	fever pitch

ich			
rich	which	sandwich	ostrich

itter			
bitter	glitter	sitter	cat litter
fitter	knitter	skitter	transmitter
fritter	litter	twitter	babysitter

ive			
dive	jive	high dive	survive
drive	live	high five	take five
five	alive	nose dive	test drive
hive	arrive	revive	deep sea dive
I've	beehive	skydive	nine to five

iver			
liver	river	sliver	downriver
quiver	shiver	deliver	upriver

Unidentified Flying Object Rap

The UFO from Mexico –
Didn't give me aggro,
Flew by full of gusto,
Had an eerie halo,
fatter than a hippo,
faster than a rhino,
quicker than a yo-yo,
brighter than a rainbow.

o

go	gusto	pogo	piano
no	halo	rhino	piccolo
so	hello	solo	potato
aggro	hero	UFO	radio
ago	hippo	yo-yo	so-and-so
ammo	info	zero	stereo
banjo	judo	buffalo	studio
bingo	lilo	calypso	to and fro
bongo	logo	commando	tornado
bravo	ludo	flamingo	touch and go
disco	macho	indigo	video
ditto	mango	inferno	volcano
dodo	metro	long ago	yes and no
echo	photo	patio	armadillo

ew

sew

oe

doe	hoe	ice floe	mistletoe
floe	toe	oboe	tale of woe
foe	woe	tiptoe	friend or foe

ough

dough	though	although	even though

ow

blow	slow	good show	shadow
bow	snow	hedgerow	shallow
crow	sow	lie low	sideshow
flow	stow	longbow	sorrow
glow	throw	marrow	window
grow	tow	meadow	bungalow
know	arrow	minnow	ebb and flow
low	below	outgrow	high and low
mow	burrow	pillow	overflow
row	crossbow	rainbow	tomorrow
show	elbow	scarecrow	wheelbarrow

oad

goad	boatload	high road	heavy load
load	by road	ring road	hit the road
road	carload	truckload	on the road
toad	cartload	unload	overload

ode

code	rode	barcode	postcode
ode	strode	explode	episode

owed

crowed	owed	snowed	elbowed
flowed	rowed	stowed	shadowed
glowed	showed	towed	overflowed
mowed	slowed	burrowed	

oard

board	clipboard	outboard	surfboard
hoard	dartboard	scoreboard	whiteboard
aboard	dashboard	skateboard	all aboard
cardboard	floorboard	snowboard	diving board
chessboard	keyboard	springboard	overboard

ard

ward	award	reward	toward

oad

broad	abroad

oared

roared	soared

ord

chord	sword	harpsichord	track record
cord	afford	spinal cord	break the
fiord	landlord	strike a chord	record
lord	record	tape-record	umbilical cord

orde

horde	Concorde

ored

bored	snored	adored	ignored
scored	stored	explored	restored

The winter stoat
runs, slim
and quick
as an eel –
its white coat
stained red
from the rabbit's
throat.

oat	boat	throat	sailboat	ferryboat
	coat	afloat	scapegoat	miss the boat
	float	cut-throat	sore throat	motorboat
	gloat	houseboat	speedboat	overcoat
	goat	lifeboat	swingboat	petticoat
	moat	raincoat	waistcoat	powerboat
	stoat	rowboat	billy goat	rock the boat

ote	dote	rote	devote	rewrote
	note	vote	promote	anecdote
	quote	wrote	remote	antidote

ob	blob	lob	sob	hobnob
	bob	mob	throb	odd job
	hob	rob	doorknob	just the job
	job	slob	good job	corn on the cob
	knob	snob	heart-throb	thingamabob

obble	bobble	gobble	hobble	wobble

uabble	squabble

O -obe to -ocky

obe			
globe	robe	earlobe	space probe
probe	strobe	microbe	wardrobe

ock			
block	mock	livestock	tick-tock
clock	rock	o'clock	unlock
cock	shock	odd sock	alarm clock
crock	sock	padlock	chock-a-block
dock	stock	peacock	chopping block
flock	airlock	punk rock	cuckoo clock
frock	deadlock	roadblock	hard as rock
knock	gridlock	shamrock	shuttlecock
lock	knock knock	sunblock	weathercock

ocks			
blocks	locks	airlocks	peacocks
clocks	mocks	dreadlocks	tick-tocks
docks	rocks	gridlocks	unlocks
flocks	shocks	odd socks	cuckoo clocks
knocks	socks	padlocks	hollyhocks

ox			
box	pox	paintbox	paradox
cox	gearbox	postbox	jack-in-the-box
fox	horsebox	toy box	
ox	lunchbox	chatterbox	
	matchbox	chicken pox	

The fat fox with yellow socks in the horsebox was a chatterbox.

ocky			
cocky	rocky	stocky	jabberwocky

ockey			
hockey	jockey	disc jockey	ice hockey

od

clod	plod	shod	tripod
cod	pod	trod	cattle prod
god	prod	hot rod	fishing rod
nod	rod	peapod	

og

bog	grog	backlog	leapfrog
clog	hog	bulldog	road hog
cog	jog	bullfrog	seadog
dog	log	guide dog	ship's log
flog	slog	hedgehog	top dog
fog	smog	hot dog	watchdog
frog	agog	lame dog	underdog

ogue

prologue	catalogue	epilogue	synagogue
analogue	dialogue	monologue	

oil

boil	soil	recoil	aerofoil
broil	spoil	tinfoil	counterfoil
coil	toil	topsoil	hydrofoil
foil	embroil	turmoil	
oil	hard-boil	uncoil	

oyal

loyal	royal	disloyal

oyle

gargoyle

oin

coin	join	adjoin	sirloin
groin	loin	rejoin	flip a coin

oint

joint	gunpoint	viewpoint	prove a point
point	high point	boiling point	score a point
appoint	low point	disappoint	starting point
checkpoint	pinpoint	focal point	beside the point

O -oise to -old

oise	noise	poise	turquoise	traffic noise

oys	boys	ploys	ballboys	enjoys
	buoys	toys	cowboys	killjoys
	joys	annoys	destroys	schoolboys

oist	foist	hoist	joist	moist

oke	bloke	poke	woke	sunstroke
	broke	smoke	awoke	cloud of smoke
	choke	spoke	breaststroke	puff of smoke
	joke	stroke	provoke	practical joke

oak	cloak	croak	oak	soak

olk	folk	yolk	old folk	townsfolk

old	bold	sold	out cold	common cold
	cold	told	retold	crock of gold
	fold	blindfold	scaffold	days of old
	gold	catch cold	stronghold	good as gold
	hold	foothold	unfold	heart of gold
	old	household	unsold	marigold
	scold	ice cold	untold	solid gold

oled	soled	cajoled	consoled	paroled

olled	polled	strolled	enrolled	steamrolled
	rolled	controlled	patrolled	unrolled

ould	mould			

The goldfish speaks

My memory lasts seven seconds –
just long enough to patrol the bowl,
arriving back where I began,
not recognizing where I am;
trapped in a never-ending loophole.

ole

dole	armhole	loophole	tadpole
hole	bargepole	manhole	as a whole
mole	beanpole	maypole	buttonhole
pole	black hole	North Pole	casserole
role	cajole	peephole	cubbyhole
sole	console	pinhole	on the whole
stole	flagpole	porthole	rigmarole
vole	insole	pothole	starring role
whole	keyhole	South Pole	totem pole

oal

foal	goal	shoal	charcoal

ol

control	patrol	self-control	remote control

oll

roll	stroll	steamroll	rock and roll
scroll	drum roll	unroll	

oul

soul	bare your soul	life and soul	body and soul

owl

bowl	fast bowl	fishbowl	sugarbowl

olt

bolt	jolt	revolt	thunderbolt
colt	volt	unbolt	

O -ome to -on

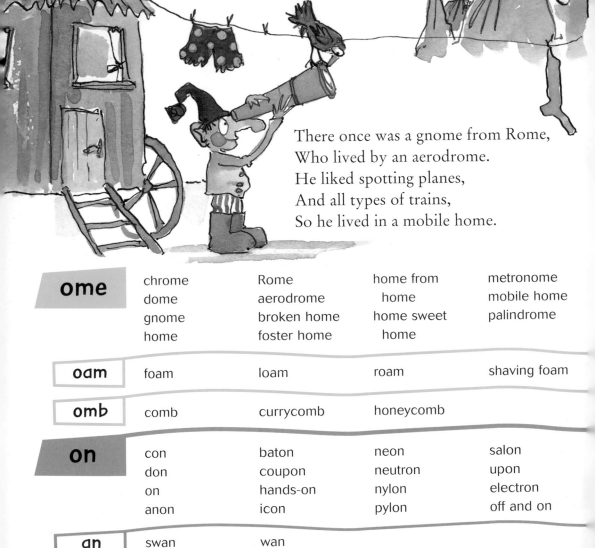

There once was a gnome from Rome,
Who lived by an aerodrome.
He liked spotting planes,
And all types of trains,
So he lived in a mobile home.

ome	chrome	Rome	home from	metronome
	dome	aerodrome	home	mobile home
	gnome	broken home	home sweet	palindrome
	home	foster home	home	

| **oam** | foam | loam | roam | shaving foam |

| **omb** | comb | currycomb | honeycomb | |

on	con	baton	neon	salon
	don	coupon	neutron	upon
	on	hands-on	nylon	electron
	anon	icon	pylon	off and on

| **an** | swan | wan | | |

| **one** | gone | scone | shone | all gone |

| **ond** | blond | fond | beyond | respond |
| | bond | pond | fishpond | vagabond |

and	wand	magic wand

onned	conned	donned

one	bone	alone	time zone	microphone
	clone	backbone	tombstone	mobile phone
	cone	cheekbone	trombone	parking zone
	drone	fishbone	war zone	rolling stone
	lone	hailstone	wishbone	saxophone
	phone	jawbone	anklebone	skin and bone
	prone	kerbstone	cobblestone	stepping-stone
	scone	ozone	collarbone	telephone
	stone	pine cone	funny bone	traffic cone
	throne	postpone	heart of stone	xylophone
	tone	shinbone	ice-cream cone	accident-prone
	zone	thighbone	megaphone	dry as a bone

ewn	sewn	hand-sewn

| **oan** | groan | loan | moan | moan and groan |

own	blown	mown	sown	unknown
	flown	own	thrown	well-known
	grown	shown	full-grown	overgrown

ong	bong	strong	headlong	sarong
	dong	throng	headstrong	sing-song
	gong	wrong	Hong Kong	so long
	long	along	love song	all along
	pong	belong	oblong	before long
	prong	ding-dong	ping-pong	in the wrong
	song	folk song	pop song	right or wrong

O -oo

oo

boo	woo	kazoo	kangaroo
coo	zoo	shampoo	peekaboo
goo	a-choo	skidoo	didgeridoo
loo	bamboo	tattoo	hullaballoo
moo	boo-hoo	voodoo	tu-whit tu-whoo
shoo	cuckoo	yoo-hoo	cock-a-doodle
too	igloo	cockatoo	doo

ew

blew	knew	stew	review
brew	mew	threw	sinew
chew	new	view	unscrew
crew	pew	askew	bird's eye view
dew	phew	brand-new	book review
drew	screw	corkscrew	interview
few	shrew	nephew	Irish stew
flew	slew	on view	point of view
grew	skew	renew	quite a few

ewe

ewe

o

do	ado	says who?	two by two
to	hairdo	to-do	well to do
two	how-to	undo	how do you do?
who	lean-to	who's who	what a to-do

oe

shoe	canoe	horseshoe	snowshoe

ou

you	thank you	after you	caribou

ough

through	see through
all through	through and
breakthrough	through

ous

rendezvous

u			
flu	guru	kung fu	Peru
gnu	Hindu	menu	tutu

ue			
blue	sue	statue	continue
clue	true	subdue	navy blue
cue	argue	tissue	overdue
due	fondue	unglue	residue
flue	pursue	untrue	bolt from the
glue	on cue	value	blue
hue	rescue	venue	out of the blue
queue	revue	avenue	red, white
rue	sky-blue	barbecue	and blue

Barbecue on the ark

The animals came in two by two,
They all queued up for the barbecue –

'Oh, after you,'
said the caribou!

'How do you do,'
said the elder ewe,

'I've a bird's eye view,'
said the cockatoo,

'What a hullaballoo,'
said the kangaroo,

But the old gnu,
as he joined the queue,
said, 'If one gnu is a gnu
then two gnus makes news.'

So he and his wife played
the didgeridoo
while the burgers sizzled
on the barbecue …

71

O -ood to -ool

ood

good	falsehood	withstood	motherhood
hood	firewood	babyhood	neighbourhood
stood	for good	brotherhood	sisterhood
wood	knighthood	fatherhood	understood
boyhood	make good	Hollywood	misunderstood
childhood	plywood	knock on wood	so far so good
driftwood	touch wood	livelihood	up to no good

ould

could	should	would

ook

book	rook	notebook	dirty look
brook	shook	outlook	off the hook
cook	took	scrapbook	overcook
crook	cookbook	sketchbook	overlook
hook	fish hook	songbook	overtook
look	handbook	textbook	second look
nook	mistook	comic book	storybook

ool

cool	spool	toadstool	lose your cool
drool	stool	whirlpool	play it cool
fool	tool	act the fool	Sunday school
pool	footstool	April fool	supercool
school	playschool	boarding school	swimming pool

oul

ghoul

uel

fuel	refuel

ule

mule	capsule	as a rule	molecule
rule	globule	golden rule	overrule
yule	schedule	minuscule	ridicule

oom

bloom	vroom	dark room	bride and
boom	zoom	heirloom	groom
broom	ballroom	houseroom	dining room
doom	bathroom	mushroom	elbow room
gloom	bedroom	playroom	gloom and
groom	bridegroom	storeroom	doom
loom	classroom	strongroom	living room
room	cloakroom	tearoom	sonic boom

ume

fume	plume	costume	perfume

oon

croon	buffoon	new moon	honeymoon
moon	cartoon	platoon	macaroon
noon	cocoon	raccoon	pretty soon
soon	festoon	teaspoon	tablespoon
spoon	full moon	too soon	wooden spoon
swoon	harpoon	twelve noon	hot-air balloon
baboon	lagoon	tycoon	man in the
balloon	maroon	typhoon	moon
bassoon	monsoon	afternoon	over the moon

une

dune	fortune
June	Neptune
prune	sand dune
tune	out of tune

The honeymoon

The raccoon and baboon
left the wedding at noon.
They dined on prunes
and macaroons
by the golden light
of the honey moon.

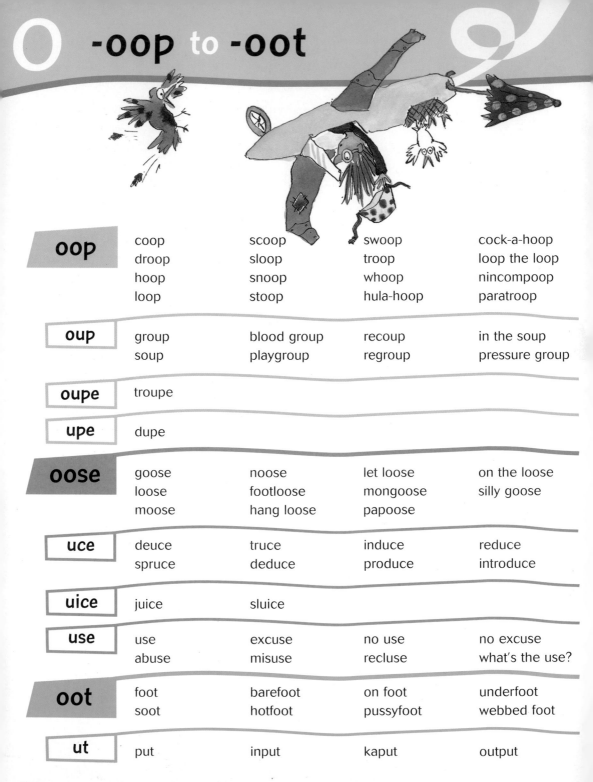

oop			
coop	scoop	swoop	cock-a-hoop
droop	sloop	troop	loop the loop
hoop	snoop	whoop	nincompoop
loop	stoop	hula-hoop	paratroop

oup			
group	blood group	recoup	in the soup
soup	playgroup	regroup	pressure group

oupe			
troupe			

upe			
dupe			

oose			
goose	noose	let loose	on the loose
loose	footloose	mongoose	silly goose
moose	hang loose	papoose	

uce			
deuce	truce	induce	reduce
spruce	deduce	produce	introduce

uice			
juice	sluice		

use			
use	excuse	no use	no excuse
abuse	misuse	recluse	what's the use?

oot			
foot	barefoot	on foot	underfoot
soot	hotfoot	pussyfoot	webbed foot

ut			
put	input	kaput	output

op

bop	prop	hilltop	tip top
chop	shop	hip hop	treetop
cop	slop	lap top	workshop
crop	stop	nonstop	bellyflop
drop	top	pit stop	lollipop
flop	big top	raindrop	mountain top
hop	bookshop	rooftop	set up shop
lop	bus stop	snowdrop	shut up shop
mop	clip-clop	sweetshop	turboprop
plop	eavesdrop	teardrop	window shop
pop	flip-flop	teashop	over the top

ope

cope	rope	antelope	periscope
grope	scope	envelope	skipping rope
hope	slope	gyroscope	stethoscope
lope	elope	horoscope	telescope
mope	tightrope	microscope	kaleidoscope
pope	towrope	not a hope	slippery slope

oap

soap	bar of soap

Fame

Could you cope –
high up, on the tightrope of fame?

Or would it be
that you'd have no hope –
blinded by your name in lights,
lost on your own slippery slope?

O -ore

ore

bore	shore	before	seashore
chore	snore	encore	therefore
core	sore	explore	all ashore
gore	store	eyesore	carnivore
lore	swore	folklore	evermore
more	tore	footsore	herbivore
ore	wore	galore	nevermore
pore	adore	ignore	sycamore
score	ashore	no more	forevermore

ar

war	all-out war	man-of-war	tug of war

aur

centaur	dinosaur	Minotaur	pterosaur

aw

caw	paw	coleslaw	outlaw
claw	raw	guffaw	pawpaw
draw	saw	hacksaw	rubbed raw
flaw	squaw	jackdaw	seesaw
gnaw	straw	jigsaw	luck of the draw
jaw	thaw	last straw	quick on the
law	chainsaw	macaw	draw

oar

boar	roar	uproar	
oar	soar		

oor

door	back door	next-door	at death's door
floor	front door	outdoor	door-to-door
poor	indoor	trapdoor	rich or poor

or

for	condor	corridor	metaphor
nor	mentor	matador	meteor

our

four	pour	downpour	troubadour

ores			
bores	scores	adores	restores
chores	shores	encores	carnivores
cores	snores	explores	herbivores
gores	sores	eyesores	pinafores
pores	stores	ignores	sycamores

ars			
wars	civil wars		

aurs			
centaurs	dinosaurs		

ause			
cause	pause	applause	lost cause

auze			
gauze			

awers			
drawers			

aws			
claws	jaws	straws	jigsaws
draws	laws	thaws	outlaws
flaws	paws	guffaws	pawpaws
gnaws	saws	jackdaws	seesaws

oars			
boars	oars	roars	soars

oors			
doors	back doors	indoors	trapdoors
floors	front doors	outdoors	out of doors

ors			
corridors	matadors	metaphors	meteors

ours			
pours	yours	troubadours	

Dinosaurs liked to roar
Until they met a meteor.

77

| ork | cork | pork | hayfork | pitchfork |
| | fork | stork | New York | knife and fork |

alk	chalk	walk	pep talk	spacewalk
	stalk	beanstalk	sleepwalk	sweet talk
	talk	catwalk	small talk	baby talk

| awk | gawk | hawk | squawk | tomahawk |

orm	form	hailstorm	platform	snowstorm
	storm	inform	rainstorm	thunderstorm
	brainstorm	perform	sandstorm	uniform

| arm | swarm | warm | lukewarm | |

orn	born	sworn	first-born	popcorn
	corn	thorn	foghorn	sweetcorn
	horn	torn	forlorn	well-worn
	morn	worn	French horn	Capricorn
	scorn	acorn	hawthorn	peppercorn
	shorn	adorn	newborn	unicorn

| aun | faun | leprechaun | | |

| awn | dawn | lawn | prawn | yawn |
| | drawn | pawn | sawn | frogspawn |

| orne | borne | airborne | seaborne | waterborne |

| ourn | mourn | | | |

Look out of your window at dawn.
There's a hoofprint, there on the lawn,
A silver hair, caught on a thorn –
You dreamt last night of a unicorn.

orse	horse	clothes horse	remorse	rocking horse
	Norse	dark horse	seahorse	Trojan horse
	carthorse	racehorse	hobbyhorse	eat like a horse

| **auce** | sauce | chocolate sauce | | |

| **oarse** | coarse | hoarse | | |

| **orce** | force | by force | divorce | reinforce |

ourse	course	golf course	off course	in due course
	concourse	main course	on course	collision course
	crash course	of course	racecourse	obstacle course

ort	fort	sport	passport	support
	port	airport	report	transport
	short	bad sport	resort	heliport
	snort	export	seaport	hold the fort
	sort	good sport	spoilsport	last resort

| **art** | thwart | wart | | |

| **aught** | caught | taught | onslaught | |
| | fraught | distraught | self-taught | |

| **aut** | taut | astronaut | juggernaut | |

ought	bought	nought	close-fought	come to nought
	brought	ought	dreadnought	deep in thought
	fought	thought	afterthought	food for thought

| **ourt** | court | forecourt | law court | tennis court |

-ose to -ost

ose	close	dose	morose	overdose

osh	gosh	nosh	posh	slosh

ash	quash	wash	carwash	whitewash
	squash	brainwash	mouthwash	

oss	boss	gloss	across	candyfloss
	cross	moss	criss-cross	doublecross
	floss	toss	albatross	motocross

ost	ghost	almost	lamppost	innermost
	host	bedpost	outpost	outermost
	most	gatepost	signpost	perfect host
	post	goalpost	utmost	deaf as a post

oast	boast	coast	roast	toast

Deaf as a post,
Grandad always said 'yes'.
A most agreeable host –
I keep his memory
warm as toast.

ot

blot	snot	high spot	apricot
clot	spot	jackpot	beauty spot
cot	swot	long shot	boiling hot
dot	tot	mascot	Camelot
got	trot	mugshot	chimneypot
hot	big shot	red-hot	coffeepot
jot	black spot	robot	flowerpot
knot	blind spot	slip knot	go to pot
lot	bloodshot	snapshot	hit the spot
not	cannot	soft spot	in a spot
plot	crackpot	sunspot	like a shot
pot	dovecot	teapot	melting pot
rot	earshot	tight spot	on the dot
Scot	forgot	topknot	on the spot
shot	fusspot	upshot	thanks a lot
slot	gunshot	white hot	forget-me-not

acht

yacht

at

squat	what	somewhat	what's what
swat	kumquat	so what?	

otion

lotion	notion	commotion	slow motion
motion	potion	devotion	magic potion

ocean

ocean

otty

dotty	knotty	potty	spotty

ouch

couch	grouch	pouch	vouch
crouch	ouch!	slouch	

O -oud to -ount

oud	cloud loud	proud shroud	aloud out loud	rain cloud thundercloud

owd	crowd	in crowd	overcrowd	follow the crowd

owed	bowed cowed	rowed vowed	wowed allowed	bow-wowed meowed

ound	bound found ground hound pound round sound wound aground around astound	background bloodhound dumbfound earthbound eastbound fairground foreground foxhound greyhound housebound icebound	newfound northbound playground profound southbound spellbound sports ground surround unsound westbound year-round	all around homeward 　bound lost and found outward bound round and 　round solid ground turnaround underground merry-go-round

owned	browned clowned	crowned downed	drowned frowned	gowned renowned

ount	count mount account	amount discount head count	keep count lose count recount	on no account out for the 　count

I can't keep count of this amount, I'll have to recount.

Don't grouse
at the woodlouse,
as it humps
and bumps
its armour-plated house.

ouse	douse	church mouse	keep house	cat and mouse
	grouse	doghouse	lighthouse	haunted house
	house	dormouse	madhouse	house to house
	louse	hothouse	warehouse	summer house

out	bout	trout	knockout	do without
	clout	about	lookout	down and out
	lout	back out	lose out	hang about
	out	blackout	pass out	in and out
	pout	breakout	shootout	inside out
	scout	check out	sold out	odd man out
	shout	chill out	throughout	roundabout
	snout	dropout	walk out	on the lookout
	spout	hang out	without	over and out
	sprout	hideout	workout	up and about

oubt	doubt	in doubt	no doubt	without a doubt

ought	drought			

ow	bow	pow	bow-wow	somehow
	brow	prow	eyebrow	anyhow
	cow	row	for now	here and now
	dhow	sow	know-how	solemn vow
	how	vow	meow	take a bow
	now	wow	now, now	any day now
	ow!	allow	pow-wow	any old how

ough	bough	plough	snowplough	

O -ower to -own

ower

cower	tower	rain shower	willpower
flower	cornflower	sunflower	cauliflower
glower	horsepower	wallflower	overpower
power	manpower	watchtower	water power
shower	Mayflower	wildflower	ivory tower

our

flour	scour	lunch hour	hour by hour
hour	sour	rush hour	on the hour
our	devour	dinner hour	sweet and sour

owl

fowl	owl	yowl	wildfowl
growl	prowl	brown owl	on the prowl
howl	scowl	night owl	wise old owl

oul

foul

owel

bowel	towel	trowel	vowel

own

brown	breakdown	lowdown	touchdown
clown	comedown	meltdown	broken-down
crown	countdown	nightgown	eiderdown
down	crackdown	put-down	hand-me-down
drown	face-down	run-down	shantytown
frown	ghost town	showdown	tumble-down
gown	home town	slowdown	up and down
town	knockdown	splashdown	upside-down
ballgown	letdown	sundown	wedding gown

oun

noun

Have you heard the upside-down bird?
Poor night owl, when out on the prowl,
you'll hear it
twoo-twit!

ows

blows	rows	bellows	rainbows
bows	shows	burrows	scarecrows
crows	slows	crossbows	shadows
flows	snows	elbows	sideshows
glows	sows	furrows	bungalows
grows	stows	hedgerows	come to blows
knows	throws	longbows	ebbs and flows
lows	tows	meadows	overflows
mows	arrows	outgrows	overthrows

oes

foes	throes	here goes!	buffaloes
goes	toes	oboes	dominoes
hoes	woes	tiptoes	volcanoes

os

banjos	pianos
bongos	radios
broncos	rodeos
hippos	so-and-sos
ponchos	stereos
rhinos	studios
yo-yos	UFOs
calypsos	videos
dynamos	
flamingos	

ose

chose	those	suppose	look down your
close	enclose	wild rose	nose
hose	expose	decompose	open and close
nose	fire hose	hold your nose	overexpose
pose	oppose	nose to nose	under your
prose	primrose	runny nose	nose
rose	propose	follow your nose	

oze

doze	froze	bulldoze	unfroze

oy			
boy	ahoy	cowboy	playboy
buoy	alloy	decoy	schoolboy
coy	annoy	destroy	tomboy
joy	ballboy	employ	corduroy
ploy	choirboy	enjoy	paperboy
toy	convoy	lifebuoy	pride and joy

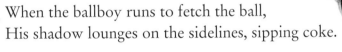

The Shadow

When the ballboy runs to fetch the ball,
His shadow lounges on the sidelines, sipping coke.

When the choirboy sings a sweet lullaby,
His shadow turns up the volume, blasting rock and roll.

When the cowboy pins on the sheriff's badge,
His shadow picks up a bag of swag.

When the tomboy climbs to the top of a tree,
Her shadow puts on a pink, frilly dress.

When the paperboy delivers the daily news,
His shadow chucks the papers into a puddle.

When the lifebuoy saves another life,
The shadow drowns itself …

ub

club	rub	tub	fox cub
cub	scrub	bathtub	hubbub
grub	shrub	bear cub	join the club
hub	snub	cherub	lion cub·
pub	stub	fan club	rub-a-dub-dub

ubble

bubble	rubble	stubble	hubble-bubble

ouble

double	deep trouble	at the double	toil and trouble
trouble	see double	double trouble	

uch

much	not much	a bit much	such and such
such	too much	pretty much	not up to much

ouch

touch	lose touch	get in touch	lose your touch
in touch	soft touch	keep in touch	out of touch

utch

clutch	crutch	Dutch	hutch

uck

buck	good luck	thunderstruck
chuck	hard luck	try your luck
cluck	moonstruck	
duck	pot luck	
luck	stagestruck	
muck	unstuck	
pluck	with luck	
puck	worse luck	
struck	horror-struck	
stuck	forklift truck	
suck	no such luck	
truck	panic-struck	
tuck	pass the buck	
yuck	push your luck	
dumbstruck	sitting duck	

uckle

buckle	knuckle	belt buckle	honeysuckle
chuckle	suckle	swashbuckle	

ud

bud	spud	rosebud	clear as mud
dud	stud	soap sud	stick-in-the-
mud	thud	tastebud	mud
scud	nose stud	chew the cud	

ood

blood	blue blood	lifeblood	flesh and blood
flood	cold blood	sweat blood	in your blood
bad blood	flash flood	chill your blood	

uddle

cuddle	huddle	muddle	puddle

ude

crude	exclude	altitude	latitude
nude	include	attitude	longitude
rude	intrude	gratitude	solitude

ewed

brewed	mewed	stewed	renewed
chewed	screwed	viewed	interviewed

ood

food	dog food	good mood	baby food
mood	fast food	seafood	in a mood
bad mood	foul mood	soul food	in the mood

ooed

booed	mooed	wooed	shampooed
cooed	shooed	boo-hooed	tattooed

ued

cued	sued	pursued	valued
glued	argued	rescued	barbecued

udge			
budge	grudge	sludge	begrudge
drudge	judge	smudge	hot fudge
fudge	nudge	trudge	misjudge

uff			
bluff	gruff	snuff	blindman's buff
buff	huff	stuff	fisticuff
cuff	puff	dandruff	huff and puff
duff	scruff	earmuff	overstuff
fluff	scuff	handcuff	powder puff

ough			
rough	enough	fair enough	enough's
tough	that's tough	sure enough	enough

ug			
bug	jug	slug	bedbug
chug	lug	smug	earplug
drug	mug	snug	humbug
dug	plug	thug	litterbug
glug	rug	tug	spark plug
hug	shrug	bear hug	unplug

Doug drives a digger.
Don't snigger,
   don't shrug,
   don't call Doug an ugly mug.
He's no smug thug –
say what you want,
he'll just shrug.
You won't see
a **bigger** figure
than Doug, on his digger.

ul

armful	graceful	restful	watchful
boastful	handful	roomful	wishful
careful	harmful	sackful	beautiful
cheerful	helpful	shameful	colourful
cupful	hopeful	skilful	pitiful
doubtful	hurtful	spoonful	plentiful
dreadful	mouthful	tearful	powerful
faithful	peaceful	useful	sorrowful
fearful	playful	wakeful	wonderful

ool

wool	lambswool	steel wool	cotton wool

ull

bull	pull	cramfull	push-pull
full	chock-full	half-full	overfull

um

chum	scum	plectrum	medium
drum	slum	spectrum	minimum
glum	strum	steel drum	museum
gum	sum	tantrum	pendulum
hum	swum	yum-yum	stadium
mum	tum	asylum	chrysanthemum
plum	album	chewing gum	fee fie fo fum
rum	eardrum	kettle drum	millennium
scrum	humdrum	maximum	

om

freedom	kingdom	stardom	wisdom

ome

come	gruesome	threesome	meddlesome
some	how come?	twosome	overcome
become	outcome	welcome	troublesome

umb

crumb	numb	thumb	Tom Thumb
dumb	plumb	succumb	deaf and dumb

umble	crumble	humble	rumble	apple crumble
	fumble	jumble	stumble	rough and
	grumble	mumble	tumble	tumble

| ummy | crummy | dummy | mummy | tummy |

ump	bump	lump	thump	speed bump
	clump	plump	trump	tree stump
	dump	pump	goosebump	bungee jump
	frump	rump	high jump	rubbish dump
	hump	slump	long jump	running jump
	jump	stump	ski jump	sugar lump

The **G**ruesome twosome

Met the awes**O**me foursome,

On the way to the rubbish dump.

The two**S**ome blew some bubble gum

Which made **E**verybody jump.

The **B**last was quite dramatic,

It tore the **U**niverse in two.

But their **M**emory lingers on

In the sha**P**e of an airborne shoe!

U -un to -ung

un

bun	run	begun	hit-and-run
fun	shun	dry run	jump the gun
gun	spun	for fun	machine gun
nun	stun	shotgun	on the run
pun	sun	what fun!	trial run

on

son	won	grandson	stetson
ton	godson	stepson	

one

done	no one	well done	everyone
none	outdone	all in one	number one
one	someone	all or none	one by one
all done	undone	anyone	over and done

unch

brunch	crunch	lunch	punch
bunch	hunch	munch	scrunch

under

blunder	thunder	blood and	loot and
plunder	under	thunder	plunder

onder

wonder	boy wonder	no wonder	nine-day wonder

ung

bung	hung	strung	wrung
clung	rung	stung	far-flung
dung	slung	sung	unsung
flung	sprung	swung	highly-strung

ongue

tongue	lost your tongue	tip of the
forked tongue	mother tongue	tongue
sharp tongue	slip of the	
hold your	tongue	
tongue		

oung

young

unk			
bunk	flunk	skunk	tree trunk
chunk	funk	slunk	
clunk	junk	sunk	
drunk	punk	trunk	
dunk	shrunk	chipmunk	

onk	
monk	

unt			
blunt	punt	stunt	manhunt
grunt	runt	bear hunt	witch hunt
hunt	shunt	fox hunt	treasure hunt

ont			
front	in front	seafront	back to front

up			
cup	dress up	make-up	toss-up
pup	fed up	mix-up	wind up
up	fry-up	pick-up	buttercup
back up	grown-up	press-up	coffee cup
break-up	hard-up	round up	cover-up
built-up	hiccup	slip-up	giddy-up
checkup	ketchup	teacup	runner-up
close-up	lock-up	throw up	washing up

My teacher has a sharp tongue –
She can cut through any nonsense!

Mum told me to hold my tongue –
But it was far too slippery!

'Have you lost your tongue?' asked the teacher.
I checked – it was still there, nestling in my mouth.

I made a slip of the tongue –
But managed not to fall over.

U -ur to -urn

ur	blur	fur	spur	demur
	cur	slur	concur	occur

er	her	per	prefer	transfer

ere	were			

ir	fir	sir	stir	astir

urk	lurk	Turk		

erk	jerk	perk	berserk	go berserk

irk	irk	quirk	shirk	smirk

ork	work	framework	teamwork	donkey work
	artwork	guesswork	waxwork	handiwork
	clockwork	homework	woodwork	hard at work
	firework	network	dirty work	overwork

url	curl	hurl	uncurl	unfurl

earl	earl	pearl	mother-of-pearl	

irl	girl	swirl	twirl	whirl

urn	burn	turn	good turn	sunburn
	spurn	urn	return	U-turn

earn	earn	learn	yearn	live and learn

ern	fern	stern	concern	

I overheard –
the cat that purred,
for it preferred
the blackest bird.
Sadly now,
the rarest bird.

urred	blurred	purred	slurred	spurred

eard	heard	unheard	overheard	have you heard?

erd	herd	nerd	cowherd	goatherd

ird	bird	firebird	rare bird	ladybird
	third	jailbird	songbird	mockingbird
	blackbird	lovebird	early bird	whirlybird
	bluebird	one-third	hummingbird	free as a bird

ord	word	last word	break your	not a word
	buzzword	password	word	word for word
	crossword	swearword	mum's the word	

urd	curd	absurd	lemon curd	

urse	curse	nurse	purse	reimburse

erse	verse	converse	diverse	reverse
	adverse	disperse	immerse	universe

orse	worse	worse and worse		

urt	blurt	curt	hurt	spurt

ert	pert	alert	desert	expert
	advert	concert	dessert	

irt	dirt	shirt	squirt	T-shirt
	flirt	skirt	sweatshirt	miniskirt

us	bus	cactus	walrus	platypus
	plus	crocus	genius	thesaurus
	pus	minus	radius	apparatus
	thus	rumpus	minibus	Diplodocus
	us	schoolbus	octopus	hocus-pocus
	bonus	virus	papyrus	hippopotamus

ous	anxious	raucous	furious	ravenous
	callous	wondrous	glorious	serious
	famous	courageous	hideous	stupendous
	gorgeous	curious	horrendous	tremendous
	jealous	dubious	ludicrous	various
	monstrous	enormous	mischievous	hilarious
	nervous	envious	numerous	ingenious
	precious	fabulous	obvious	mysterious

uss	fuss	suss	discuss	kick up a fuss

use	fuse	use	confuse	excuse
	muse	accuse	defuse	peruse
	ruse	amuse	enthuse	refuse

ews	news	stews	cashews	interviews

oos	boos	zoos	tattoos	kangaroos

ose	choose	lose	whose	win or lose

ush			
blush	hush	shush	hairbrush
brush	lush	slush	hush-hush
crush	mush	thrush	paintbrush
flush	plush	bulrush	songthrush
gush	rush	gold rush	toothbrush

usk			
busk	husk	rusk	corn husk
dusk	musk	tusk	dawn to dusk

ust			
bust	must	disgust	stardust
crust	rust	go bust	unjust
dust	thrust	gold dust	bite the dust
gust	trust	mistrust	dry as dust
just	adjust	sawdust	like gold dust

ussed			
bussed	fussed	discussed	nonplussed

ut			
but	rut	doughnut	walnut
cut	scut	haircut	coconut
glut	shut	half-shut	halibut
gut	smut	peanut	hazelnut
hut	strut	rebut	in a rut
jut	beechnut	shortcut	undercut
nut	chestnut	tough nut	uppercut
phut	clear-cut	tut-tut	open and shut

utt			
butt	mutt	putt	ugly mutt

Danny's dog
was an ugly mutt –
Too much hair
in need of a cut.
Shaved him bald
Like a coconut ...
Tut. Tut. Tut!

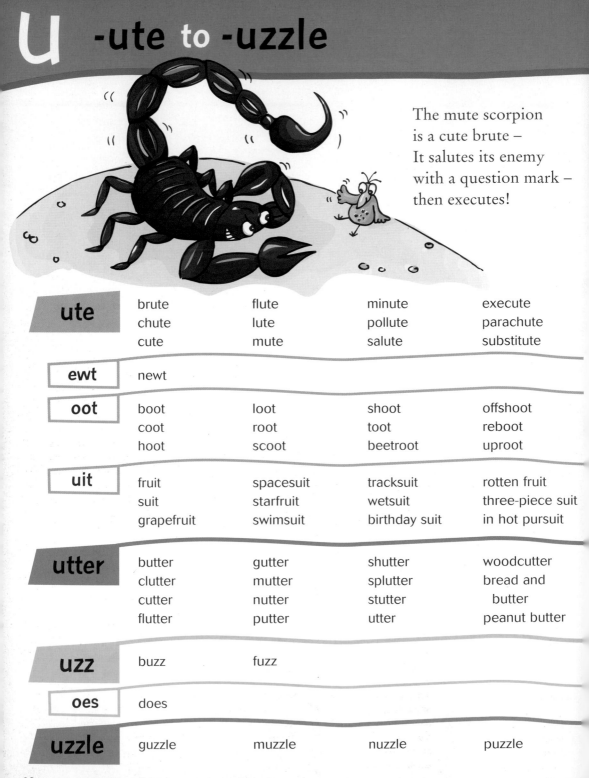

The mute scorpion
is a cute brute –
It salutes its enemy
with a question mark –
then executes!

ute				
brute	flute	minute	execute
chute	lute	pollute	parachute
cute	mute	salute	substitute

ewt				
newt			

oot				
boot	loot	shoot	offshoot
coot	root	toot	reboot
hoot	scoot	beetroot	uproot

uit				
fruit	spacesuit	tracksuit	rotten fruit
suit	starfruit	wetsuit	three-piece suit
grapefruit	swimsuit	birthday suit	in hot pursuit

utter				
butter	gutter	shutter	woodcutter
clutter	mutter	splutter	bread and
cutter	nutter	stutter	butter
flutter	putter	utter	peanut butter

uzz		
buzz	fuzz	

oes	
does	

uzzle				
guzzle	muzzle	nuzzle	puzzle

Index

arrow / -o	61
arrowhead / -ed	35
arrows / -ows	85
art / -art	23
artefact / -act	11
artwork / -urk	94
ascend / -end	41
ascent / -ent	41
ash / -ash	23
ashore / -ore	76
aside / -ide	48
ask / -ask	23
askew / -oo	70
asleep / -eep	38
assassinate / -ate	25
asterisk / -isk	58
astir / -ur	94
astound / -ound	82
astride / -ide	48
astronaut / -ort	79
asylum / -um	90
at / -at	24
ate / -ate	25
athlete / -eat	32
Atlantic / -antic	21
atmosphere / -ear	31
attach / -atch	24
attack / -ack	10
attacked / -act	11
attacks / -acks	11
attend / -end	41
attic / -ick	46
attitude / -ude	88
attract / -act	11
autograph / -arf	22
automatic / -ick	46
automobile / -eal	30
avenue / -oo	71
await / -ate	25
awake / -ake	16
award / -oard	62
aware / -air	15
away / -ay	27
awhile / -ile	52
awoke / -oke	66
axe / -acks	11
axis / -iss	58
aye aye / -i	45

baa / -a	8
babble / -abble	8
baboon / -oon	73
babyhood / -ood	72
babysat / -at	24
babysit / -it	59
babysitter / -itter	60
back / -ack	10
backache / -ake	16
backbend / -end	41
backbone / -one	69
backed / -act	11
backfire / -ire	57
background / -ound	82
backhand / -and	19
backlash / -ash	23
backlog / -og	65
backpack / -ack	10
backpacked / -act	11
backpacks / -acks	11
backs / -acks	11
backseat / -eat	32
backside / -ide	48
backstage / -age	13
backstreet / -eat	32
backtrack / -ack	10
backtracked / -act	11
backtracks / -acks	11
bad / -ad	12
bag / -ag	13
bagpipe / -ipe	57
baguette / -et	44
bail / -ale	14
bait / -ate	25
bake / -ake	16
balderdash / -ash	23
bale / -ale	14
ball / -all	17
ballboy / -oy	86
ballboys / -oise	66
ballet / -ay	27
ballgown / -own	84
balloon / -oon	73
ballroom / -oom	73
bamboo / -oo	70
ban / -an	18
band / -and	19
bandit / -it	59
bandstand / -and	19
bane / -ane	20

bang / -ang	20
bangle / -angle	20
banjo / -o	61
banjos / -ows	85
bank / -ank	21
banned / -and	19
bap / -ap	21
bar / -a	8
barbecue / -oo	71
barbecued / -ude	88
barcode / -oad	62
bare / -air	15
bareback / -ack	10
barefaced / -aced	9
barefoot / -oot	74
bargepole / -ole	67
bark / -ark	22
barred / -ard	22
barricade / -ade	12
base / -ace	9
baseball / -all	17
bash / -ash	23
basic / -ick	46
bask / -ask	23
basket / -it	59
basketball / -all	17
bassoon / -oon	73
bat / -at	24
bathroom / -oom	73
bathtub / -ub	87
baton / -on	68
batter / -atter	26
battle / -attle	26
battleship / -ip	57
batty / -atty	26
bawl / -all	17
bay / -ay	27
bays / -aze	28
bazaar / -a	8
BC / -e	29
be / -e	29
bead / -eed	36
beak / -eek	37
beam / -eam	30
bean / -een	37
beanbag / -ag	13
beanfeast / -east	32
beanpole / -ole	67
beanstalk / -ork	78
bear / -air	15
bearskin / -in	54
beast / -east	32
beat / -eat	32

beater / -eater	33
beautiful / -ul	90
became / -ame	18
beck / -eck	33
become / -um	90
bed / -ed	35
bedbug / -ug	89
bedpost / -ost	80
bedroom / -oom	73
bedside / -ide	48
bedspread / -ed	35
bedstead / -ed	35
bedtime / -ime	54
bee / -e	29
beechnut / -ut	97
beef / -eaf	30
beefsteak / -ake	16
beehive / -ive	60
beeline / -ine	55
been / -een	37
beep / -eep	38
beer / -ear	31
bees / -ees	38
beeswax / -acks	11
beetroot / -ute	98
before / -ore	76
beforehand / -and	19
befriend / -end	41
beg / -eg	39
began / -an	18
begin / -in	54
begrudge / -udge	89
begun / -un	92
behalf / -arf	22
behave / -ave	27
behead / -ed	35
behind / -ind	55
belief / -eaf	30
believe / -eve	44
bell / -ell	39
bellow / -ello	39
bellows / -ows	85
bellyache / -ake	16
bellyflop / -op	75
belong / -ong	69
below / -o	61
belt / -elt	40
bench / -ench	40
bend / -end	41
bent / -ent	41
bequest / -est	43
beret / -ay	27
berry / -erry	42

Word	Rhyme	Page
berserk	-urk	94
bespatter	-atter	26
best	-est	43
bet	-et	44
Bethlehem	-em	40
betray	-ay	27
betrayed	-ade	12
betrays	-aze	28
between	-een	37
beware	-air	15
bewitch	-itch	60
beyond	-ond	69
bib	-ib	46
bid	-id	47
biff	-iff	49
biffed	-ift	50
big	-ig	50
bigwig	-ig	50
bike	-ike	51
bill	-ill	52
billionaire	-air	15
bin	-in	54
bind	-ind	55
binge	-inge	56
bingo	-o	61
bionic	-ick	46
biosphere	-ear	31
bird	-urred	95
birdcage	-age	13
birdcall	-all	17
birdseed	-eed	36
birthday	-ay	27
birthdays	-aze	28
birthplace	-ace	9
biscuit	-it	59
bit	-it	59
bite	-ight	51
bitter	-itter	60
bittersweet	-eat	32
blab	-ab	8
black	-ack	10
blackberry	-erry	42
blackbird	-urred	95
blacked	-act	11
blackhead	-ed	35
blackmail	-ale	14
blackout	-out	83
blade	-ade	12
blame	-ame	18
blank	-ank	21
blare	-air	15
blast	-ast	24
blaze	-aze	28
bleak	-eek	37
bleat	-eat	32
bled	-ed	35
bleed	-eed	36
bleep	-eep	38
blend	-end	41
blender	-ender	41
bless	-ess	42
blessed	-est	43
blew	-oo	70
blind	-ind	55
blindfold	-old	66
blink	-ink	56
blip	-ip	57
bliss	-iss	58
blob	-ob	63
block	-ock	64
blocks	-ocks	64
bloke	-oke	66
blond	-ond	69
blood	-ud	88
bloodhound	-ound	82
bloodshed	-ed	35
bloodshot	-ot	81
bloodstream	-eam	30
bloom	-oom	73
blot	-ot	81
blow	-o	61
blown	-one	69
blows	-ows	85
blue	-oo	71
bluebell	-ell	39
blueberry	-erry	42
bluebird	-urred	95
blueprint	-int	57
bluetit	-it	59
bluff	-uff	89
blunder	-under	92
blunt	-unt	93
blur	-ur	94
blurred	-urred	95
blurt	-urt	96
blush	-ush	97
boar	-ore	76
board	-oard	62
boars	-ores	77
boast	-ost	80
boastful	-ul	90
boat	-oat	63
boatload	-oad	62
bob	-ob	63
bobble	-obble	63
bobsled	-ed	35
bobsleigh	-ay	27
bodyguard	-ard	22
bog	-og	65
boil	-oil	65
bold	-old	66
bolt	-olt	67
bombard	-ard	22
bombshell	-ell	39
bond	-ond	69
bone	-one	69
bonfire	-ire	57
bong	-ong	69
bongo	-o	61
bongos	-ows	85
bonus	-us	96
boo	-oo	70
booed	-ude	88
boo-hoo	-oo	70
boo-hooed	-ude	88
book	-ook	72
bookcase	-ace	9
bookmark	-ark	22
bookshop	-op	75
bookstall	-all	17
boom	-oom	73
boomerang	-ang	20
boos	-use	96
boot	-ute	98
bop	-op	75
borderline	-ine	55
bore	-ore	76
bored	-oard	62
bores	-ores	77
boring	-ing	56
born	-orn	78
borne	-orn	78
boss	-oss	80
bottleneck	-eck	33
bottlenecks	-ecks	34
bough	-ow	83
bought	-ort	79
bound	-ound	82
bouquet	-ay	27
bout	-out	83
boutique	-eek	37
bow	-o	61
bow	-ow	83
bowed	-oud	82
bowel	-owl	84
bowl	-ole	67
bows	-ows	85
bow-wow	-ow	83
bow-wowed	-oud	82
box	-ocks	64
boy	-oy	86
boyfriend	-end	41
boyhood	-ood	72
boys	-oise	66
brace	-ace	9
braced	-aced	9
bracelet	-it	59
brag	-ag	13
braid	-ade	12
brain	-ane	20
brainstorm	-orm	78
brainwash	-osh	80
brainwave	-ave	27
brake	-ake	16
bran	-an	18
brand	-and	19
brandish	-ish	58
brash	-ash	23
brass	-ass	24
brat	-at	24
brave	-ave	27
bravo	-o	61
brawl	-all	17
bray	-ay	27
brayed	-ade	12
brays	-aze	28
bread	-ed	35
break	-ake	16
breakdown	-own	84
breakneck	-eck	33
breakout	-out	83
breakthrough	-oo	70
breast	-est	43
breaststroke	-oke	66
bred	-ed	35
breed	-eed	36
breeze	-ees	38
breezy	-easy	32
brew	-oo	70
brewed	-ude	88
bric-a-brac	-ack	10
brick	-ick	46
bricks	-icks	47
bride	-ide	48
bridegroom	-oom	73
bridesmaid	-ade	12
bridge	-idge	49
brief	-eaf	30
bright	-ight	51
brill	-ill	52
brim	-im	53
brine	-ine	55

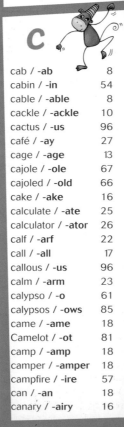

C

chatterbox / -ocks	64	chitchat / -at	24	clinch / -inch	55	coil / -oil	65
chatty / -atty	26	chlorine / -een	37	cling / -ing	56	coin / -oin	65
cheap / -eep	25	choirboy / -oy	86	clink / -ink	56	cold / -old	66
cheapskate / -ate	25	choke / -oke	66	clip / -ip	57	coleslaw / -ore	76
cheat / -eat	32	choose / -use	96	clipboard / -oard	62	collarbone / -one	69
check / -eck	33	chop / -op	75	clip-clop / -op	75	collect / -ect	34
checked / -ect	34	chopstick / -ick	46	clique / -eek	37	colourblind / -ind	55
checklist / -ist	58	chopsticks / -icks	47	cloak / -oke	66	colourful / -ul	90
checkmate / -ate	25	chord / -oard	62	cloakroom / -oom	73	colt / -olt	67
checkpoint / -oint	65	chore / -ore	76	clock / -ock	64	comb / -ome	68
checks / -ecks	34	chores / -ores	77	clocks / -ocks	64	combat / -at	24
checkup / -up	93	chose / -ows	85	clockwise / -ies	49	combine / -ine	55
cheek / -eek	37	chow mein / -ane	20	clockwork / -urk	94	come / -um	90
cheekbone / -one	69	chrome / -ome	68	clod / -od	65	comedown / -own	84
cheep / -eep	38	chrysalis / -iss	58	clog / -og	65	comic / -ick	46
cheer / -ear	31	chuck / -uck	87	clone / -one	69	comics / -icks	47
cheerful / -ul	90	chuckle / -uckle	88	close / -ose	80	commando / -o	61
cheese / -ees	38	chug / -ug	89	close / -ows	85	commonplace / -ace	9
cheesecake / -ake	16	chum / -um	90	clot / -ot	81	commotion / -otion	81
cheetah / -eater	33	chunk / -unk	93	clothesline / -ine	55	communicate / -ate	25
cheque / -eck	33	chute / -ute	98	clothing / -ing	56	compact / -act	11
cherry / -erry	42	circuit / -it	59	cloud / -oud	82	compare / -air	15
cherub / -ub	87	citadel / -ell	39	clout / -out	83	compete / -eat	32
chess / -ess	42	citizen / -en	40	cloverleaf / -eaf	30	complain / -ane	20
chessboard / -oard	62	citizenship / -ip	57	clown / -own	84	complete / -eat	32
chest / -est	43	clackity-clack / -ack	10	clowned / -ound	82	complicate / -ate	25
chestnut / -ut	97	clad / -ad	12	club / -ub	87	compliment / -ent	41
chew / -oo	70	claim / -ame	18	cluck / -uck	87	con / -on	68
chewed / -ude	88	clam / -am	17	clue / -oo	71	conceal / -eal	30
chick / -ick	46	clamp / -amp	18	clump / -ump	91	concentrate / -ate	25
chickpea / -e	29	clan / -an	18	clung / -ung	92	concern / -urn	94
chickpeas / -ees	38	clang / -ang	20	clunk / -unk	93	concert / -urt	96
chicks / -icks	47	clank / -ank	21	clutch / -uch	87	concise / -ice	46
chief / -eaf	30	clap / -ap	21	clutter / -utter	98	Concorde / -oard	62
chihuahua / -a	8	clarinet / -et	44	coarse / -orse	79	concourse / -orse	79
child / -ild	52	clash / -ash	23	coast / -ost	80	concur / -ur	94
childhood / -ood	72	clasp / -asp	23	coastguard / -ard	22	condor / -ore	76
childlike / -ike	51	class / -ass	24	coastline / -ine	55	cone / -one	69
chill / -ill	52	classed / -ast	24	coat / -oat	63	confess / -ess	42
chilli / -illy	53	classroom / -oom	73	cobblestone / -one	69	confessed / -est	43
chilly / -illy	53	clatter / -atter	26	cock / -ock	64	confiscate / -ate	25
chime / -ime	54	claw / -ore	76	cockatoo / -oo	70	confuse / -use	96
chimney / -e	29	claws / -ores	77	cockleshell / -ell	39	conman / -an	18
chimneys / -ees	38	clay / -ay	27	cockpit / -it	59	connect / -ect	34
chimneypot / -ot	81	clean / -een	37	cocky / -ocky	64	conned / -ond	69
chimpanzee / -e	29	clear / -ear	31	coconut / -ut	97	conquest / -est	43
chimpanzees / -ees	38	clementine / -een	37	cocoon / -oon	73	consent / -ent	41
chin / -in	54	clench / -ench	40	cod / -od	65	console / -ole	67
Chinese / -ees	38	click / -ick	46	code / -oad	62	consoled / -old	66
chink / -ink	56	clicks / -icks	47	coffee / -e	29	contain / -ane	20
chinwag / -ag	13	cliff / -iff	49	coffeepot / -ot	81	content / -ent	41
chip / -ip	57	climax / -acks	11	coffin / -in	54	contest / -est	43
chipmunk / -unk	93	climb / -ime	54	cog / -og	65	continue / -oo	71

contraband / -and	19
contract / -act	11
contrary / -airy	16
contrast / -ast	24
control / -ole	67
controlled / -old	66
converse / -urse	95
convoy / -oy	86
coo / -oo	70
cooed / -ude	88
cook / -ook	72
cookbook / -ook	72
cool / -ool	72
coop / -oop	74
cooperate / -ate	25
coot / -ute	98
cop / -op	75
cope / -ope	75
copycat / -at	24
copyright / -ight	51
cord / -oard	62
corduroy / -oy	86
core / -ore	76
cores / -ores	77
cork / -ork	78
corkscrew / -oo	70
corn / -orn	78
cornflower / -ower	84
correct / -ect	34
corridor / -ore	76
corridors / -ores	77
costume / -oom	73
cot / -ot	81
couch / -ouch	81
could / -ood	72
count / -ount	82
countdown / -own	84
counterfoil / -oil	65
countryside / -ide	48
coupon / -on	68
courageous / -us	96
courgette / -et	44
course / -orse	79
court / -ort	79
cow / -ow	83
cowardice / -iss	58
cowbell / -ell	39
cowboy / -oy	86
cowboys / -oise	66
cowed / -oud	82
cower / -ower	84
cowherd / -urred	95
cowpat / -at	24

cowslip / -ip	57
cox / -ocks	64
coy / -oy	86
crab / -ab	8
crabby / -abby	8
crack / -ack	10
crackdown / -own	84
cracked / -act	11
crackle / -ackle	10
crackpot / -ot	81
cracks / -acks	11
craft / -aft	13
crag / -ag	13
cram / -am	17
cramfull / -ul	90
cramp / -amp	18
crane / -ane	20
crank / -ank	21
crankshaft / -aft	13
crash / -ash	23
crash-land / -and	19
crate / -ate	25
crater / -ator	26
crave / -ave	27
crawl / -all	17
craze / -aze	28
creak / -eek	37
cream / -eam	30
crease / -eece	36
creased / -east	32
create / -ate	25
creator / -ator	26
creed / -eed	36
creek / -eek	37
creep / -eep	38
crept / -ept	42
cress / -ess	42
crest / -est	43
crew / -oo	70
crib / -ib	46
cricket / -it	59
cried / -ide	48
cries / -ies	49
crime / -ime	54
cringe / -inge	56
crispbread / -ed	35
croak / -oke	66
crock / -ock	64
crocodile / -ile	52
crocus / -us	96
crone / -one	69
crook / -ook	72
croon / -oon	73

crop / -op	75
croquette / -et	44
cross / -oss	80
crossbar / -a	8
crossbow / -o	61
crossbows / -ows	85
crosspatch / -atch	24
crossword / -urred	95
crouch / -ouch	81
crow / -o	61
crowbar / -a	8
crowd / -oud	82
crowed / -oad	62
crown / -own	84
crowned / -ound	82
crows / -ows	85
crude / -ude	88
crumb / -um	90
crumble / -umble	91
crummy / -ummy	91
crunch / -unch	92
crush / -ush	97
crust / -ust	97
crutch / -uch	87
cry / -i	45
cub / -ub	87
cubbyhole / -ole	67
cuckoo / -oo	70
cuddle / -uddle	88
cue / -oo	71
cued / -ude	88
cuff / -uff	89
cuisine / -een	37
cul-de-sac / -ack	10
culprit / -it	59
cunning / -ing	56
cup / -up	93
cupful / -ul	90
cur / -ur	94
curd / -urred	95
curious / -us	96
curl / -url	94
currycomb / -ome	68
curse / -urse	95
curt / -urt	96
cut / -ut	97
cute / -ute	98
cut-rate / -ate	25
cutter / -utter	98
cyclist / -ist	58
Czech / -eck	33

d

dab / -ab	8
dabble / -abble	8
dad / -ad	12
daffodil / -ill	52
daft / -aft	13
dairy / -airy	16
dale / -ale	14
dam / -am	17
damp / -amp	18
damper / -amper	18
dance / -ance	19
dandruff / -uff	89
dangle / -angle	20
dank / -ank	21
dare / -air	15
dark / -ark	22
dart / -art	23
dartboard / -oard	62
dash / -ash	23
dashboard / -oard	62
database / -ace	9
date / -ate	25
dawn / -orn	78
day / -ay	27
daybreak / -ake	16
daydream / -eam	30
day-dreaming / -ing	56
daylight / -ight	51
days / -aze	28
daytime / -ime	54
daze / -aze	28
DC / -e	29
dead / -ed	35
deadbeat / -eat	32
deadlock / -ock	64
deadpan / -an	18
deal / -eal	30
dear / -ear	31
deathbed / -ed	35
debate / -ate	25
decade / -ade	12
decay / -ay	27
decayed / -ade	12
deceased / -east	32
deceive / -eve	44
decide / -ide	48
deck / -eck	33
decks / -ecks	34
declare / -air	15

decompose / -ows	85	deuce / -oose	74
decorate / -ate	25	devote / -oat	63
decoy / -oy	86	devotion / -otion	81
decrease / -eece	36	devour / -ower	84
decreased / -east	32	dew / -oo	70
decrees / -ees	38	dhow / -ow	83
deduce / -oose	74	diagram / -am	17
deed / -eed	36	dial / -ile	52
deep / -eep	38	dialect / -ect	34
deer / -ear	31	dialogue / -og	65
deface / -ace	9	dice / -ice	46
defaced / -aced	9	dictator / -ator	26
defeat / -eat	32	did / -id	47
defence / -ence	40	diddle / -iddle	47
defend / -end	41	didgeridoo / -oo	70
defender / -ender	41	die / -i	45
defuse / -use	96	died / -ide	48
degree / -e	29	dies / -ies	49
degrees / -ees	38	dig / -ig	50
delay / -ay	27	digest / -est	43
delayed / -ade	12	digress / -ess	42
delays / -aze	28	digressed / -est	43
delete / -eat	32	dill / -ill	52
deliberate / -ate	25	dilly-dally / -alley	17
delight / -ight	51	dim / -im	53
deliver / -iver	60	dime / -ime	54
deliveryman / -an	18	dine / -ine	55
demonstrate / -ate	25	dined / -ind	55
demur / -ur	94	dingbat / -at	24
den / -en	40	ding-dong / -ong	69
denied / -ide	48	dinnertime / -ime	54
denim / -im	53	dinosaur / -ore	76
dense / -ence	40	dinosaurs / -ores	77
dent / -ent	41	dip / -ip	57
deny / -i	45	Diplodocus / -us	96
depart / -art	23	dire / -ipe	57
depend / -end	41	direct / -ect	34
depress / -ess	42	dirt / -urt	96
depressed / -est	43	disagree / -e	29
descend / -end	41	disagreed / -eed	36
descent / -ent	41	disagrees / -ees	38
desert / -urt	96	disappear / -ear	31
design / -ine	55	disappoint / -oint	65
desire / -ire	57	disarm / -arm	23
despair / -air	15	disbelieve / -eve	44
dessert / -urt	96	disco / -o	61
destroy / -oy	86	disconnect / -ect	34
destroys / -oise	66	discontent / -ent	41
detach / -atch	24	discotheque / -eck	33
detail / -ale	14	discount / -ount	82
detect / -ect	34	discreet / -eat	32
detest / -est	43	discuss / -us	96
detonate / -ate	25	discussed / -ust	97

disease / -ees	38	doors / -ores	77
disgrace / -ace	9	doorway / -ay	27
disgraced / -aced	9	doorways / -aze	28
disguise / -ies	49	dormouse / -ouse	83
disgust / -ust	97	dose / -ose	80
dish / -ish	58	dot / -ot	81
disk / -isk	58	dote / -oat	63
dislike / -ike	51	dotty / -otty	81
disloyal / -oil	65	double / -ubble	87
dismiss / -iss	58	doublecross / -oss	80
dismissed / -ist	58	doubt / -out	83
disobey / -ay	27	doubtful / -ul	90
disobeyed / -ade	12	dough / -o	61
disperse / -urse	95	doughnut / -ut	97
displaced / -aced	9	douse / -ouse	83
displayed / -ade	12	dovecot / -ot	81
disrespect / -ect	34	down / -own	84
distract / -act	11	downcast / -ast	24
distraught / -ort	79	downed / -ound	82
distress / -ess	42	downfall / -all	17
distressed / -est	43	downhill / -ill	52
ditch / -itch	60	downpour / -ore	76
ditto / -o	61	downriver / -iver	60
dive / -ive	60	downstream / -eam	30
diverse / -urse	95	doze / -ows	85
divide / -ide	48	drab / -ab	8
divine / -ine	55	drag / -ag	13
divorce / -orse	79	dragnet / -et	44
do / -oo	70	dragonflies / -ies	49
dock / -ock	64	dragonfly / -i	45
docks / -ocks	64	drain / -ane	20
dodo / -o	61	drainpipe / -ipe	57
doe / -o	61	drake / -ake	16
does / -uzz	98	drank / -ank	21
dog / -og	65	drape / -ape	21
doghouse / -ouse	83	draught / -aft	13
doing / -ing	56	draw / -ore	76
dole / -ole	67	drawback / -ack	10
dolphin / -in	54	drawbridge / -idge	49
dome / -ome	68	drawers / -ores	77
dominoes / -ows	85	drawl / -all	17
don / -on	68	drawn / -orn	78
done / -un	92	draws / -ores	77
dong / -ong	69	dread / -ed	35
donkey / -e	29	dreadful / -ul	90
donkeys / -ees	38	dreadlocks / -ocks	64
donned / -ond	69	dreadnought / -ort	79
doom / -oom	73	dream / -eam	30
door jamb / -am	17	dreamland / -and	19
door / -ore	76	dredge / -edge	35
doorbell / -ell	39	dreg / -eg	39
doorknob / -ob	63	drench / -ench	40
doormat / -at	24	dress / -ess	42

footsore / -ore	76	
footstool / -ool	72	
footwear / -air	15	
for / -ore	76	
forbid / -id	47	
force / -orse	79	
ford / -oard	62	
forecast / -ast	24	
forecourt / -ort	79	
foreground / -ound	82	
forehand / -and	19	
forehead / -ed	35	
foreseen / -een	37	
forevermore / -ore	76	
forgave / -ave	27	
forget / -et	44	
forget-me-not / -ot	81	
forgot / -ot	81	
fork / -ork	78	
forlorn / -orn	78	
form / -orm	78	
fort / -ort	79	
forthright / -ight	51	
fortnight / -ight	51	
fortune / -oon	73	
fought / -ort	79	
foul / -owl	84	
found / -ound	82	
four / -ore	76	
fourteen / -een	37	
fowl / -owl	84	
fox / -ocks	64	
foxhound / -ound	82	
fragile / -ile	52	
fragment / -ent	41	
frail / -ale	14	
frame / -ame	18	
framework / -urk	94	
France / -ance	19	
frank / -ank	21	
frantic / -antic	21	
fraught / -ort	79	
fray / -ay	27	
frayed / -ade	12	
frays / -aze	28	
freak / -eek	37	
free / -e	29	
freed / -eed	36	
freedom / -um	90	
freefall / -all	17	
freehand / -and	19	
freelance / -ance	19	
frees / -ees	38	

freestyle / -ile	52
freewheel / -eal	30
freewheeling / -ing	56
freeze / -ees	38
freight / -ate	25
French / -ench	40
fresh / -esh	42
fret / -et	44
Friday / -ay	27
fridge / -idge	49
fried / -ide	48
friend / -end	41
friendship / -ip	57
fries / -ies	49
fright / -ight	51
frill / -ill	52
frilly / -illy	53
fringe / -inge	56
fritter / -itter	60
frizz / -is	58
frock / -ock	64
frog / -og	65
frogmarch / -arch	22
frogspawn / -orn	78
front / -unt	93
frontier / -ear	31
frostbite / -ight	51
frown / -own	84
frowned / -ound	82
froze / -ows	85
fruit / -ute	98
fruitcake / -ake	16
frump / -ump	91
frustrate / -ate	25
fry / -i	45
fudge / -udge	89
fuel / -ool	72
fulfil / -ill	52
full / -ul	90
fumble / -umble	91
fume / -oom	73
fun / -un	92
funfair / -air	15
funk / -unk	93
fur / -ur	94
furious / -us	96
furrows / -ows	85
fuse / -use	96
fuss / -us	96
fussed / -ust	97
fusspot / -ot	81
fuzz / -uzz	98

g

gabble / -abble	8
gadget / -it	59
gag / -ag	13
gaga / -a	8
gale / -ale	14
galley / -alley	17
galore / -ore	76
game / -ame	18
gang / -ang	20
gangplank / -ank	21
gangway / -ay	27
gap / -ap	21
gape / -ape	21
gargoyle / -oil	65
garlic / -ick	46
gash / -ash	23
gasp / -asp	23
gate / -ate	25
gatecrash / -ash	23
gatepost / -ost	80
gauze / -ores	77
gave / -ave	27
gawk / -ork	78
gaze / -aze	28
gear / -ear	31
gearbox / -ocks	64
gel / -ell	39
gem / -em	40
gender / -ender	41
gene / -een	37
genie / -e	29
genius / -us	96
germinate / -ate	25
get / -et	44
ghost / -ost	80
ghostlike / -ike	51
ghoul / -ool	72
gift / -ift	50
gig / -ig	50
gigantic / -antic	21
giggle / -iggle	50
gill / -ill	52
gimmick / -ick	46
gimmicks / -icks	47
gingerbread / -ed	35
giraffe / -arf	22
girl / -url	94
girlfriend / -end	41
gist / -ist	58
glad / -ad	12

glade / -ade	12
glance / -ance	19
gland / -and	19
glare / -air	15
glass / -ass	24
glaze / -aze	28
gleam / -eam	30
glean / -een	37
glee / -e	29
glen / -en	40
glide / -ide	48
glint / -int	57
glitch / -itch	60
glitter / -itter	60
gloat / -oat	63
globe / -obe	64
globule / -ool	72
gloom / -oom	73
glorious / -us	96
gloss / -oss	80
glow / -o	61
glowed / -oad	62
glower / -ower	84
glows / -ows	85
glue / -oo	71
glued / -ude	88
glug / -ug	89
glum / -um	90
glut / -ut	97
gnash / -ash	23
gnat / -at	24
gnaw / -ore	76
gnaws / -ores	77
gnome / -ome	68
gnu / -oo	71
go / -o	61
goad / -oad	62
goal / -ole	67
goalpost / -ost	80
goat / -oat	63
goatherd / -urred	95
gobble / -obble	63
goblin / -in	54
god / -od	65
godchild / -ild	52
godson / -un	92
goes / -ows	85
go-kart / -art	23
gold / -old	66
goldfish / -ish	58
gondolier / -ear	31
gone / -on	68
gong / -ong	69

goo / -oo	70	greenfly / -i	45
good / -ood	72	greet / -eat	32
goodbye / -i	45	gremlin / -in	54
goodwill / -ill	52	grenade / -ade	12
goose / -oose	74	grew / -oo	70
gooseberry / -erry	42	grey / -ay	27
goosebump / -ump	91	greyhound / -ound	82
gooseflesh / -esh	42	grid / -id	47
gore / -ore	76	griddle / -iddle	47
gores / -ores	77	gridlock / -ock	64
gorgeous / -us	96	gridlocks / -ocks	64
gosh / -osh	80	grief / -eaf	30
gossip / -ip	57	grieve / -eve	44
got / -ot	81	grill / -ill	52
gown / -own	84	grim / -im	53
gowned / -ound	82	grime / -ime	54
grab / -ab	8	grin / -in	54
grace / -ace	9	grind / -ind	55
graced / -aced	9	grip / -ip	57
graceful / -ul	90	gripe / -ipe	57
grade / -ade	12	grit / -it	59
graffiti / -e	29	groan / -one	69
graft / -aft	13	grog / -og	65
grain / -ane	20	groin / -oin	65
gram / -am	17	groom / -oom	73
gran / -an	18	grope / -ope	75
grand / -and	19	grouch / -ouch	81
granddad / -ad	12	ground / -ound	82
grandma / -a	8	groundsheet / -eat	32
grandpa / -a	8	group / -oop	74
grandson / -un	92	grouse / -ouse	83
grandstand / -and	19	grow / -o	61
grants / -ance	19	growl / -owl	84
grape / -ape	21	grown / -one	69
grapefruit / -ute	98	grows / -ows	85
grapevine / -ine	55	grub / -ub	87
graph / -arf	22	grudge / -udge	89
grasp / -asp	23	gruesome / -um	90
grass / -ass	24	gruff / -uff	89
grassed / -ast	24	grumble / -umble	91
grassland / -and	19	grunt / -unt	93
grate / -ate	25	guarantee / -e	29
grater / -ator	26	guaranteed / -eed	36
gratitude / -ude	88	guarantees / -ees	38
grave / -ave	27	guard / -ard	22
graveyard / -ard	22	guess / -ess	42
graze / -aze	28	guessed / -est	43
grease / -eece	36	guesswork / -urk	94
greased / -east	32	guest / -est	43
Greece / -eece	36	guffaw / -ore	76
greed / -eed	36	guffaws / -ores	77
Greek / -eek	37	guide / -ide	48
green / -een	37	guideline / -ine	55

guillotine / -een	37
guilt / -ilt	53
guise / -ies	49
guitar / -a	8
gum / -um	90
gun / -un	92
gunfire / -ire	57
gunpoint / -oint	65
gunshot / -ot	81
guru / -oo	71
gush / -ush	97
gust / -ust	97
gusto / -o	61
gut / -ut	97
gutter / -utter	98
guttersnipe / -ipe	57
guy / -i	45
guzzle / -uzzle	98
gym / -im	53
gymnastics / -icks	47
gyroscope / -ope	75

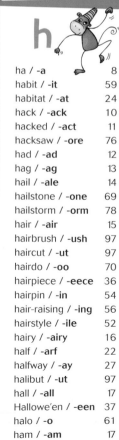

h

ha / -a	8
habit / -it	59
habitat / -at	24
hack / -ack	10
hacked / -act	11
hacksaw / -ore	76
had / -ad	12
hag / -ag	13
hail / -ale	14
hailstone / -one	69
hailstorm / -orm	78
hair / -air	15
hairbrush / -ush	97
haircut / -ut	97
hairdo / -oo	70
hairpiece / -eece	36
hairpin / -in	54
hair-raising / -ing	56
hairstyle / -ile	52
hairy / -airy	16
half / -arf	22
halfway / -ay	27
halibut / -ut	97
hall / -all	17
Hallowe'en / -een	37
halo / -o	61
ham / -am	17

hamper / -amper	18
hand / -and	19
handbag / -ag	13
handbook / -ook	72
handbrake / -ake	16
handcuff / -uff	89
handful / -ul	90
handicap / -ap	21
handiwork / -urk	95
handkerchief / -eaf	30
handlebar / -a	8
handmade / -ade	12
handset / -et	44
handshake / -ake	16
handstand / -and	19
handyman / -an	18
hang / -ang	20
hard / -ard	22
hardhat / -at	24
hardship / -ip	57
hardware / -air	15
hare / -air	15
hark / -ark	22
harm / -arm	23
harmful / -ul	90
harpoon / -oon	73
harpsichord / -oard	62
hash / -ash	23
haste / -aced	9
hat / -at	24
hatch / -atch	24
hate / -ate	25
haul / -all	17
hawk / -ork	78
hawthorn / -orn	78
hay / -ay	27
hayfork / -ork	78
haystack / -ack	10
haystacks / -acks	11
haywire / -ire	57
haze / -aze	28
hazelnut / -ut	97
he / -e	29
head / -ed	35
headache / -ake	16
headdress / -ess	42
headlight / -ight	51
headline / -ine	55
headlong / -ong	69
headset / -et	44
headscarf / -arf	22
headstand / -and	19
headstrong / -ong	69

i

misunderstood/-ood	72	motorway / -ay	27
misuse / -oose	74	mould / -old	66
mite / -ight	51	mount / -ount	82
mix / -icks	47	mountaineer / -ear	31
moan / -one	69	mourn / -orn	78

misunderstood/-ood 72
misuse / -oose 74
mite / -ight 51
mix / -icks 47
moan / -one 69
moat / -oat 63
mob / -ob 63
mobile / -ile 52
mobilize / -ies 49
mock / -ock 64
mockingbird /-urred 95
mocks / -ocks 64
modem / -em 40
moist / -oist 66
mole / -ole 67
molecule / -ool 72
molehill / -ill 52
Monday / -ay 27
money / -e 29
mongoose / -oose 74
monk / -unk 93
monkey / -e 29
monkeys / -ees 38
monologue / -og 65
monorail / -ale 14
monsoon / -oon 73
monstrous / -us 96
moo / -oo 70
mood / -ude 88
mooed / -ude 88
moon / -oon 73
moonbeam / -eam 30
moonlight / -ight 51
moonlit / -it 59
moonshine / -ine 55
moonstruck / -uck 87
moose / -oose 74
mop / -op 75
mope / -ope 75
moped / -ed 35
more / -ore 76
morn / -orn 78
morose / -ose 80
mosaic / -ick 46
moss / -oss 80
most / -ost 80
motel / -ell 39
motherhood / -ood 72
motif / -eaf 30
motion / -otion 81
motocross / -oss 80
motorbike / -ike 51
motorboat / -oat 63

motorway / -ay 27
mould / -old 66
mount / -ount 82
mountaineer / -ear 31
mourn / -orn 78
mousetrap / -ap 21
mouthful / -ul 90
mouthwash / -osh 80
mow / -o 61
mowed / -oad 62
mown / -one 69
mows / -ows 85
much / -uch 87
muck / -uck 87
mud / -ud 88
muddle / -uddle 88
mudguard / -ard 22
muffin / -in 54
mug / -ug 89
mugshot / -ot 81
mule / -ool 72
multiplied / -ide 48
multiplies / -ies 49
multiply / -i 45
mum / -um 90
mumble / -umble 91
mummy / -ummy 91
munch / -unch 92
muse / -use 96
museum / -um 90
mush / -ush 97
mushroom / -oom 73
music / -ick 46
musk / -usk 97
musketeer / -ear 31
must / -ust 97
mute / -ute 98
mutt / -ut 97
mutter / -utter 98
muzzle / -uzzle 98
my / -i 45
mysterious / -us 96
mystified / -ide 48
mystify / -i 45
mystique / -eek 37

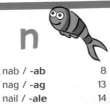

n

nab / -ab 8
nag / -ag 13
nail / -ale 14

name / -ame 18
namesake / -ake 16
nan / -an 18
nap / -ap 21
nape / -ape 21
narrator / -ator 26
natter / -atter 26
natty / -atty 26
navigator / -ator 26
near / -ear 31
nearby / -i 45
neat / -eat 32
neater / -eater 33
neck / -eck 33
necks / -ecks 34
nectarine / -een 37
need / -eed 36
neglect / -ect 34
neigh / -ay 27
neighbourhood/-ood 72
neighed / -ade 12
neon / -on 68
nephew / -oo 70
Neptune / -oon 73
nerd / -urred 95
nervous / -us 96
nest / -est 43
net / -et 44
netball / -all 17
nettle / -ettle 44
network / -urk 94
neutron / -on 68
nevermore / -ore 76
New York / -ork 78
new / -oo 70
newborn / -orn 78
newfound / -ound 82
newlywed / -ed 35
news / -use 96
newsflash / -ash 23
newsprint / -int 57
newt / -ute 98
nibble / -ibble 46
nice / -ice 46
nickname / -ame 18
nicks / -icks 47
niece / -eece 36
niggle / -iggle 50
night / -ight 51
nightcap / -ap 21
nightdress / -ess 42
nightfall / -all 17
nightgown / -own 84

nightingale / -ale 14
nightmare / -air 15
nightwear / -air 15
nil / -ill 52
Nile / -ile 52
nincompoop / -oop 74
nine / -ine 55
nineteen / -een 37
nip / -ip 57
nit / -it 59
nitpick / -ick 46
no / -o 61
nod / -od 65
noise / -oise 66
nomad / -ad 12
none / -un 92
nonetheless / -ess 42
nonplussed / -ust 97
nonsense / -ence 40
non-slip / -ip 57
non-stick / -ick 46
nonstop / -op 75
nook / -ook 72
noon / -oon 73
noose / -oose 74
nor / -ore 76
Norse / -orse 79
northbound / -ound 82
northeast / -east 32
northwest / -est 43
nose / -ows 85
nosebleed / -eed 36
nosering / -ing 56
nosh / -osh 80
not / -ot 81
note / -oat 63
notebook / -ook 72
nothing / -ing 56
notion / -otion 81
nought / -ort 79
noun / -own 84
novice / -iss 58
now / -ow 83
nowadays / -aze 28
nowhere / -air 15
nude / -ude 88
nudge / -udge 89
nugget / -it 59
numb / -um 90
numerous / -us 96
nun / -un 92
nurse / -urse 95
nut / -ut 97

nutcase / -ace 9
nutmeg / -eg 39
nutshell / -ell 39
nutter / -utter 98
nuzzle / -uzzle 98
nylon / -on 68

O

oak / -oke 66
oar / -ore 76
oars / -ores 77
oatcake / -ake 16
oatmeal / -eal 30
obey / -ay 27
obeyed / -ade 12
object / -ect 34
oblique / -eek 37
oblong / -ong 69
oboe / -o 61
oboes / -ows 85
obsessed / -est 43
obvious / -us 96
occur / -ur 94
ocean / -otion 81
o'clock / -ock 64
octopus / -us 96
oddball / -all 17
ode / -oad 62
offence / -ence 40
offend / -end 41
offender / -ender 41
offhand / -and 19
office / -iss 58
offshoot / -ute 98
offside / -ide 48
offstage / -age 13
oil / -oil 65
okay / -ay 27
old / -old 66
omelette / -et 44
on / -on 68
one / -un 92
onslaught / -ort 79
ooze / -use 96
opaque / -ake 16
operate / -ate 25
operator / -ator 26
oppose / -ows 85
oppress / -ess 42

orangeade / -ade 12
orang-utan / -an 18
orbit / -it 59
ordeal / -eal 30
ore / -ore 76
organic / -ick 46
origin / -in 54
ornament / -ent 41
ostrich / -itch 60
ouch! / -ouch 81
ought / -ort 79
our / -ower 84
out / -out 83
outback / -ack 10
outboard / -oard 62
outbreak / -ake 16
outcast / -ast 24
outclass / -ass 24
outcome / -um 90
outcry / -i 45
outdone / -un 92
outdoor / -ore 76
outdoors / -ores 77
outermost / -ost 80
outfit / -it 59
outgrow / -o 61
outgrows / -ows 85
outlast / -ast 24
outlaw / -ore 76
outlaws / -ores 77
outline / -ine 55
outlined / -ind 55
outlook / -ook 72
outpaced / -aced 9
outpost / -ost 80
output / -oot 74
outrage / -age 13
outright / -ight 51
outshine / -ine 55
outside / -ide 48
outsize / -ies 49
outsmart / -art 23
outspread / -ed 35
outweighed / -ade 12
outwit / -it 59
overact / -act 11
overall / -all 17
overarm / -arm 23
overate / -ate 25
overboard / -oard 62
overcame / -ame 18
overcast / -ast 24

overcoat / -oat 63
overcome / -um 90
overcook / -ook 72
overcrowd / -oud 82
overdose / -ose 80
overdressed / -est 43
overdue / -oo 71
overeat / -eat 32
overexpose / -ows 85
overfed / -ed 35
overfill / -ill 52
overflow / -o 61
overflowed / -oad 62
overflows / -ows 85
overfull / -ul 90
overgrown / -one 69
overhang / -ang 20
overhaul / -all 17
overhead / -ed 35
overhear / -ear 31
overheard / -urred 95
overheat / -eat 32
overkill / -ill 52
overland / -and 19
overlap / -ap 21
overleaf / -eaf 30
overload / -oad 62
overlook / -ook 72
overnight / -ight 51
overpaid / -ade 12
overpower / -ower 84
overreact / -act 11
overripe / -ipe 57
overrule / -ool 72
overseas / -ees 38
oversee / -e 29
oversees / -ees 38
oversight / -ight 51
oversleep / -eep 38
overslept / -ept 42
overspend / -end 41
overspent / -ent 41
overstepped / -ept 42
overstuff / -uff 89
overtake / -ake 16
overthrows / -ows 85
overtime / -ime 54
overtook / -ook 72
overweight / -ate 25
overwork / -urk 94
ow! / -ow 83
owed / -oad 62
owl / -owl 84

own / -one 69
ox / -ocks 64
ozone / -one 69

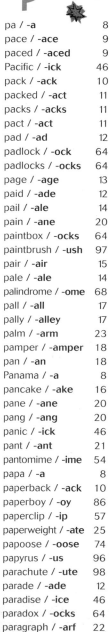

P

pa / -a 8
pace / -ace 9
paced / -aced 9
Pacific / -ick 46
pack / -ack 10
packed / -act 11
packs / -acks 11
pact / -act 11
pad / -ad 12
padlock / -ock 64
padlocks / -ocks 64
page / -age 13
paid / -ade 12
pail / -ale 14
pain / -ane 20
paintbox / -ocks 64
paintbrush / -ush 97
pair / -air 15
pale / -ale 14
palindrome / -ome 68
pall / -all 17
pally / -alley 17
palm / -arm 23
pamper / -amper 18
pan / -an 18
Panama / -a 8
pancake / -ake 16
pane / -ane 20
pang / -ang 20
panic / -ick 46
pant / -ant 21
pantomime / -ime 54
papa / -a 8
paperback / -ack 10
paperboy / -oy 86
paperclip / -ip 57
paperweight / -ate 25
papoose / -oose 74
papyrus / -us 96
parachute / -ute 98
parade / -ade 12
paradise / -ice 46
paradox / -ocks 64
paragraph / -arf 22

plume / -oom	73
plump / -ump	91
plunder / -under	92
plus / -us	96
plush / -ush	97
plywood / -ood	72
pocket / -it	59
pocketknife / -ife	49
pod / -od	65
pogo / -o	61
point / -oint	65
poise / -oise	66
poke / -oke	66
pole / -ole	67
poleaxe / -acks	11
police / -eece	36
policed / -east	32
polite / -ight	51
polled / -old	66
pollute / -ute	98
ponchos / -ows	85
pond / -ond	69
pong / -ong	69
ponytail / -ale	14
pool / -ool	72
poor / -ore	76
pop / -op	75
popcorn / -orn	78
pope / -ope	75
porcupine / -ine	55
pore / -ore	76
pores / -ores	77
pork / -ork	78
porridge / -idge	49
port / -ort	79
portcullis / -iss	58
porthole / -ole	67
portrait / -ate	25
portrayed / -ade	12
pose / -ows	85
posh / -osh	80
posse / -e	29
possess / -ess	42
possessed / -est	43
post / -ost	80
postbag / -ag	13
postbox / -ocks	64
postcard / -ard	22
postcode / -oad	62
postmark / -ark	22
postpone / -one	69
pot / -ot	81
potato / -o	61

pothole / -ole	67
potion / -otion	81
potty / -otty	81
pouch / -ouch	81
pound / -ound	82
pour / -ore	76
pours / -ores	77
pout / -out	83
pow / -ow	83
power / -ower	84
powerboat / -oat	63
powerful / -ul	90
pow-wow / -ow	83
pox / -ocks	64
practice / -iss	58
prairie / -airy	16
praise / -aze	28
pram / -am	17
prance / -ance	19
prang / -ang	20
prank / -ank	21
prawn / -orn	78
pray / -ay	27
prayed / -ade	12
prays / -aze	28
precious / -us	96
precipice / -iss	58
precise / -ice	46
preen / -een	37
prefect / -ect	34
prefer / -ur	94
prehistoric / -ick	46
premiership / -ip	57
prepare / -air	15
present / -ent	41
press / -ess	42
pressed / -est	43
pretence / -ence	40
pretend / -end	41
prevent / -ent	41
prey / -ay	27
preyed / -ade	12
price / -ice	46
pricks / -icks	47
pride / -ide	48
prim / -im	53
primate / -ate	25
prime / -ime	54
primrose / -ows	85
princess / -ess	42
print / -int	57
prise / -ies	49
prize / -ies	49

probe / -obe	64
proceed / -eed	36
proclaim / -ame	18
prod / -od	65
produce / -oose	74
profile / -ile	52
profound / -ound	82
program / -am	17
progress / -ess	42
progressed / -est	43
prohibit / -it	59
project / -ect	34
prologue / -og	65
promote / -oat	63
prone / -one	69
prong / -ong	69
proofread / -eed	36
prop / -op	75
propel / -ell	39
propose / -ows	85
prose / -ows	85
protect / -ect	34
protest / -est	43
prototype / -ipe	57
proud / -oud	82
provoke / -oke	66
prow / -ow	83
prowl / -owl	84
prune / -oon	73
pry / -i	45
psalm / -arm	23
pseudonym / -im	53
pterosaur / -ore	76
pub / -ub	87
public / -ick	46
puck / -uck	87
pudding / -ing	56
puddle / -uddle	88
puff / -uff	89
puffin / -in	54
pull / -ul	90
pump / -ump	91
pumpkin / -in	54
pun / -un	92
punch / -unch	92
punchbag / -ag	13
punchline / -ine	55
punish / -ish	58
punk / -unk	93
punt / -unt	93
pup / -up	93
puppet / -it	59
puppeteer / -ear	31

purred / -urred	95
purse / -urse	95
pursue / -oo	71
pursued / -ude	88
pus / -us	96
pushchair / -air	15
pussycat / -at	24
pussyfoot / -oot	74
put / -oot	74
putt / -ut	97
putter / -utter	98
puzzle / -uzzle	98
pylon / -on	68
pyramid / -id	47

quack / -ack	10
quacked / -act	11
quacks / -acks	11
quadrangle / -angle	20
quadruped / -ed	35
quagmire / -ire	57
quail / -ale	14
quake / -ake	16
qualm / -arm	23
quarantine / -een	37
quartet / -et	44
quash / -osh	80
quay / -e	29
queasy / -easy	32
queen / -een	37
quell / -ell	39
quench / -ench	40
quest / -est	43
queue / -oo	71
quibble / -ibble	46
quick / -ick	46
quicksand / -and	19
quid / -id	47
quill / -ill	52
quilt / -ilt	53
quintet / -et	44
quip / -ip	57
quirk / -urk	94
quit / -it	59
quite / -ight	51
quiver / -iver	60
quiz / -is	58
quote / -oat	63

r

rabbi / -i	45
rabbit / -it	59
raccoon / -oon	73
race / -ace	9
racecourse / -orse	79
raced / -aced	9
racehorse / -orse	79
racetrack / -ack	10
racing / -ing	56
rack / -ack	10
racket / -it	59
racks / -acks	11
radar / -a	8
radiator / -ator	26
radio / -o	61
radios / -ows	85
radius / -us	96
raft / -aft	13
rag / -ag	13
rage / -age	13
raid / -ade	12
rail / -ale	14
railing / -ing	56
railway / -ay	27
railways / -aze	28
rain / -ane	20
rainbow / -o	61
rainbows / -ows	85
raincoat / -oat	63
raindrop / -op	75
rainfall / -all	17
rainstorm / -orm	78
rainswept / -ept	42
raise / -aze	28
rake / -ake	16
rally / -alley	17
ram / -am	17
ramp / -amp	18
rampage / -age	13
ramshackle / -ackle	10
ran / -an	18
rang / -ang	20
ransack / -ack	10
ransacked / -act	11
ransacks / -acks	11
rant / -ant	21
rap / -ap	21
rapid / -id	47
rare / -air	15
rash / -ash	23

rasp / -asp	23
raspberry / -erry	42
rat / -at	24
ratbag / -ag	13
rate / -ate	25
rattle / -attle	26
rattlesnake / -ake	16
ratty / -atty	26
raucous / -us	96
rave / -ave	27
ravenous / -us	96
ravine / -een	37
raw / -ore	76
ray / -ay	27
rays / -aze	28
raze / -aze	28
react / -act	11
read / -ed	35
read / -eed	36
readily / -illy	53
real / -eal	30
realize / -ies	49
reap / -eep	38
reappear / -ear	31
rear / -ear	31
rebel / -ell	39
reboot / -ute	98
rebut / -ut	97
recall / -all	17
recap / -ap	21
receive / -eve	44
recipe / -e	29
recite / -ight	51
reclaim / -ame	18
recluse / -oose	74
recognize / -ies	49
recoil / -oil	65
recommend / -end	41
record / -oard	62
recount / -ount	82
recoup / -oop	74
rectangle / -angle	20
red / -ed	35
redeem / -eam	30
redhead / -ed	35
reduce / -oose	74
reed / -eed	36
reef / -eaf	30
reek / -eek	37
reel / -eal	30
referee / -e	29
refereed / -eed	36
referees / -ees	38

refill / -ill	52
reflect / -ect	34
refresh / -esh	42
refrigerate / -ate	25
refuel / -ool	72
refugee / -e	29
refugees / -ees	38
refuse / -use	96
regret / -et	44
regroup / -oop	74
reign / -ane	20
reimburse / -urse	95
rein / -ane	20
reindeer / -ear	31
reinforce / -orse	79
reject / -ect	34
rejoin / -oin	65
relax / -acks	11
release / -eece	36
released / -east	32
relent / -ent	41
relied / -ide	48
relief / -eaf	30
relieve / -eve	44
rely / -i	45
remain / -ane	20
remark / -ark	22
remind / -ind	55
remorse / -orse	79
remote / -oat	63
rendezvous / -oo	70
renew / -oo	70
renewed / -ude	88
renowned / -ound	82
rent / -ent	41
repaid / -ade	12
repair / -air	15
repeat / -eat	32
rephrase / aze	28
replace / -ace	9
replaced / -aced	9
replayed / ade	12
replied / -ide	48
replies / -ies	49
reply / -i	45
report / -ort	79
represent / -ent	41
repress / -ess	42
reprieve / -eve	44
reprint / -int	57
reptile / -ile	52
request / -est	43
reread / -eed	36

rescue / -oo	71
rescued / -ude	88
resent / -ent	41
residue / -oo	71
resign / -ine	55
resist / -ist	58
resort / -ort	79
respect / -ect	34
respond / -ond	69
rest / -est	43
restful / -ul	90
restored / -oard	62
restores / -ores	77
retell / -ell	39
rethink / -ink	56
retold / -old	66
retrace / -ace	9
retraced / -aced	9
retreat / -eat	32
retrieve / -eve	44
return / -urn	94
reveal / -eal	30
reverberate / -ate	25
revere / -ear	31
reverse / -urse	95
review / -oo	70
revive / -ive	60
revolt / -olt	67
revue / -oo	71
reward / -oard	62
rewind / -ind	55
rewrote / -oat	63
rhino / -o	61
rhinos / -ows	85
rhyme / -ime	54
rib / -ib	46
rice / -ice	46
rich / -itch	60
ricochet / -ay	27
rid / -id	47
riddle / -iddle	47
ride / -ide	48
ridge / -idge	49
ridicule / -ool	72
rift / -ift	50
right / -ight	51
rigid / -id	47
rigmarole / -ole	67
rim / -im	53
rind / -ind	55
ring / -ing	56
rink / -ink	56
RIP / -e	29

rip / -ip 57
ripe / -ipe 57
rise / -ies 49
risk / -isk 58
river / -iver 60
riverside / -ide 48
road / -oad 62
roadblock / -ock 64
roadside / -ide 48
roam / -ome 68
roar / -ore 76
roared / -oard 62
roaring / -ing 56
roars / -ores 77
roast / -ost 80
rob / -ob 63
robe / -obe 64
robin / -in 54
robot / -ot 81
rock / -ock 64
rockabye / -i 45
rocket / -it 59
rocks / -ocks 64
rocky / -ocky 64
rod / -od 65
rode / -oad 62
rodeos / -ows 85
role / -ole 67
roll / -ole 67
rolled / -old 66
romantic / -antic 21
Rome / -ome 68
rooftop / -op 75
rook / -ook 72
room / -oom 73
roomful / -ul 90
root / -ute 98
rope / -ope 75
rose / -ows 85
rosebud / -ud 88
rosette / -et 44
rot / -ot 81
rotate / -ate 25
rote / -oat 63
rough / -uff 89
roulette / -et 44
round / -ound 82
roundabout / -out 83
Roundhead / -ed 35
routine / -een 37
row / -o 61
row / -ow 83
rowboat / -oat 63

rowed / -oad 62
rowed / -oud 82
rows / -ows 85
royal / -oil 65
RSVP / -e 29
rub / -ub 87
rub-a-dub-dub / -ub 87
rubbish / -ish 58
rubble / -ubble 87
rucksack / -ack 10
rucksacks / -acks 11
rude / -ude 88
rue / -oo 71
rug / -ug 89
ruin / -in 54
rule / -ool 72
rum / -um 90
rumble / -umble 91
rump / -ump 91
rumpsteak / -ake 16
rumpus / -us 96
run / -un 92
runaway / -ay 27
runaways / -aze 28
rung / -ung 92
running / -ing 56
runt / -unt 93
runway / -ay 27
runways / -aze 28
rupee / -e 29
rupees / -ees 38
ruse / -use 96
rush / -ush 97
rusk / -usk 97
rust / -ust 97
rut / -ut 97
rye / -i 45

S

sable / -able 8
sac / -ack 10
sachet / -ay 27
sack / -ack 10
sacked / -act 11
sackful / -ul 90
sacks / -acks 11
sacrifice / -ice 46
sad / -ad 12
saddlebag / -ag 13
sag / -ag 13

said / -ed 35
sail / -ale 14
sailboat / -oat 63
sake / -ake 16
sale / -ale 14
salon / -on 68
salute / -ute 98
same / -ame 18
sand / -and 19
sandbag / -ag 13
sandbank / -ank 21
sandman / -an 18
sandstorm / -orm 78
sandwich / -itch 60
sane / -ane 20
sang / -ang 20
sank / -ank 21
sap / -ap 21
sapphire / -ire 57
sardine / -een 37
sarong / -ong 69
sash / -ash 23
sat / -at 24
satellite / -ight 51
satin / -in 54
satisfied / -ide 48
satisfy / -i 45
Saturday / -ay 27
sauce / -orse 79
save / -ave 27
saw / -ore 76
sawdust / -ust 97
sawmill / -ill 52
sawn / -orn 78
saws / -ores 77
sax / -acks 11
saxophone / -one 69
say / -ay 27
scab / -ab 8
scaffold / -old 66
scale / -ale 14
scallywag / -ag 13
scam / -am 17
scamp / -amp 18
scamper / -amper 18
scan / -an 18
scanned / -and 19
scant / -ant 21
scapegoat / -oat 63
scar / -a 8
scare / -air 15
scarecrow / -o 61
scarecrows / -ows 85

scarf / -arf 22
scarred / -ard 22
scary / -airy 16
scatter / -atter 26
scatterbrain / -ane 20
scatty / -atty 26
schedule / -ool 72
scene / -een 37
scent / -ent 41
scheme / -eam 30
school / -ool 72
schoolboy / -oy 86
schoolboys / -oise 66
schoolbus / -us 96
schoolmate / -ate 25
sci-fi / -i 45
scold / -old 66
scone / -on 68
scone / -one 69
scoop / -oop 74
scoot / -ute 98
scope / -ope 75
score / -ore 76
scoreboard / -oard 62
scorecard / -ard 22
scored / -oard 62
scores / -ores 77
scorn / -orn 78
Scot / -ot 81
scour / -ower 84
scout / -out 83
scowl / -owl 84
scrabble / -abble 8
scram / -am 17
scrap / -ap 21
scrapbook / -ook 72
scrape / -ape 21
scrapyard / -ard 22
scratch / -atch 24
scrawl / -all 17
scream / -eam 30
screen / -een 37
screw / -oo 70
screwed / -ude 88
scribble / -ibble 46
scroll / -ole 67
scrub / -ub 87
scruff / -uff 89
scrum / -um 90
scrunch / -unch 92
scud / -ud 88
scuff / -uff 89
scum / -um 90

scut / -ut	97	settle / -ettle	44
sea / -e	29	seventeen / -een	37
seaborne / -orn	78	severe / -ear	31
seadog / -og	65	sew / -o	61
seafood / -ude	88	sewn / -one	69
seahorse / -orse	79	shabby / -abby	8
seal / -eal	30	shack / -ack	10
seam / -eam	30	shackle / -ackle	10
seaport / -ort	79	shacks / -acks	11
searchlight / -ight	51	shade / -ade	12
seas / -ees	38	shadow / -o	61
seascape / -ape	21	shadowed / -oad	62
seashell / -ell	39	shadows / -ows	85
seashore / -ore	76	shaft / -aft	13
seasick / -ick	46	shake / -ake	16
seaside / -ide	48	shallow / -o	61
seat / -eat	32	sham / -am	17
seatbelt / -elt	40	shame / -ame	18
seaweed / -eed	36	shamefaced / -aced	9
secondhand / -and	19	shameful / -ul	90
secret / -it	59	shampoo / -oo	70
sect / -ect	34	shampooed / -ude	88
see / -e	29	shamrock / -ock	64
seed / -eed	36	shantytown / -own	84
seek / -eek	37	shape / -ape	21
seem / -eam	30	shard / -ard	22
seen / -een	37	share / -air	15
seep / -eep	38	shark / -ark	22
sees / -ees	38	shatter / -atter	26
seesaw / -ore	76	shave / -ave	27
seesaws / -ores	77	shawl / -all	17
seize / -ees	38	she / -e	29
select / -ect	34	sheaf / -eaf	30
self-defence / -ence	40	shear / -ear	31
self-esteem / -eam	30	shed / -ed	35
selfish / -ish	58	sheen / -een	37
self-service / -iss	58	sheep / -eep	38
sell / -ell	39	sheepish / -ish	58
send / -end	41	sheepskin / -in	54
sender / -ender	41	sheer / -ear	31
sense / -ence	40	sheet / -eat	32
sent / -ent	41	shell / -ell	39
separate / -ate	25	shellfish / -ish	58
sequin / -in	54	shift / -ift	50
serene / -een	37	shin / -in	54
serious / -us	96	shinbone / -one	69
service / -iss	58	shine / -ine	55
serviette / -et	44	ship / -ip	57
set / -et	44	shipmate / -ate	25
setback / -ack	10	shipshape / -ape	21
setbacks / -acks	11	shipwreck / -eck	33
settee / -e	29	shipwrecked / -ect	34
		shipwrecks / -ecks	34

shirk / -urk	94	Sicily / -illy	53
shirt / -urt	96	sick / -ick	46
shiver / -iver	60	sickbed / -ed	35
shoal / -ole	67	side / -ide	48
shock / -ock	64	sideshow / -o	61
shocks / -ocks	64	sideshows / -ows	85
shockwave / -ave	27	sidestepped / -ept	42
shod / -od	65	sidetrack / -ack	10
shoe / -oo	70	sidetracked / -act	11
shoelace / -ace	9	sidetracks / -acks	11
shoeshine / -ine	55	sideways / -aze	28
shone / -on	68	sift / -ift	50
shoo / -oo	70	sigh / -i	45
shooed / -ude	88	sighed / -ide	48
shook / -ook	72	sighs / -ies	49
shoot / -ute	98	sight / -ight	51
shootout / -out	83	sightsee / -e	29
shop / -op	75	sightsees / -ees	38
shoplift / -ift	50	sign / -ine	55
shore / -ore	76	signed / -ind	55
shores / -ores	77	signpost / -ost	80
shorn / -orn	78	silhouette / -et	44
short / -ort	79	sill / -ill	52
shortbread / -ed	35	silly / -illy	53
shortcut / -ut	97	silly-billy / -illy	53
shot / -ot	81	simplify / -i	45
shotgun / -un	92	simulator / -ator	26
should / -ood	72	sin / -in	54
shout / -out	83	Sinbad / -ad	12
show / -o	61	sincere / -ear	31
showbiz / -is	58	sinew / -oo	70
showdown / -own	84	sing / -ing	56
showed / -oad	62	singe / -inge	56
shower / -ower	84	sink / -ink	56
shown / -one	69	sip / -ip	57
shows / -ows	85	sir / -ur	94
shrank / -ank	21	sirloin / -oin	65
shred / -ed	35	sisterhood / -ood	72
shrew / -oo	70	sit / -it	59
shriek / -eek	37	sitar / -a	8
shrill / -ill	52	site / -ight	51
shrink / -ink	56	sitter / -itter	60
shroud / -oud	82	sitting / -ing	56
shrub / -ub	87	six / -icks	47
shrug / -ug	89	sixteen / -een	37
shrunk / -unk	93	size / -ies	49
shun / -un	92	skate / -ate	25
shunt / -unt	93	skateboard / -oard	62
shush / -ush	97	skater / -ator	26
shut / -ut	97	skating / -ing	56
shutter / -utter	98	sketch / -etch	44
shuttlecock / -ock	64	sketchbook / -ook	72
shy / -i	45	skew / -oo	70

stretch / -etch 44
stride / -ide 48
strike / -ike 51
string / -ing 56
strip / -ip 57
stripe / -ipe 57
strobe / -obe 64
strode / -oad 62
stroke / -oke 66
stroll / -ole 67
strolled / -old 66
strong / -ong 69
stronghold / -old 66
strongroom / -oom 73
struck / -uck 87
strum / -um 90
strung / -ung 92
strut / -ut 97
stub / -ub 87
stubble / -ubble 87
stuck / -uck 87
stud / -ud 88
studio / -o 61
studios / -ows 85
stuff / -uff 89
stumble / -umble 91
stump / -ump 91
stun / -un 92
stung / -ung 92
stunning / -ing 56
stunt / -unt 93
stupendous / -us 96
stupify / -i 45
stutter / -utter 98
sty / -i 45
style / -ile 52
subdue / -oo 71
subject / -ect 34
submarine / -een 37
substitute / -ute 98
subtract / -act 11
subway / -ay 27
subways / -aze 28
succeed / -eed 36
success / -ess 42
succumb / -um 90
such / -uch 87
suck / -uck 87
suckle / -uckle 88
sue / -oo 71
sued / -ude 88
suede / -ade 12
sugarbowl / -ole 67

suggest / -est 43
suit / -ute 98
suitcase / -ace 9
sum / -um 90
summertime / -ime 54
summit / -it 59
sun / -un 92
sunbeam / -eam 30
sunblock / -ock 64
sunburn / -urn 94
sundress / -ess 42
Sunday / -ay 27
Sundays / -aze 28
sundial / -ile 52
sundown / -own 84
sundress / -ess 42
sunflower / -ower 84
sung / -ung 92
sunhat / -at 24
sunk / -unk 93
sunlight / -ight 51
sunlit / -it 59
sunrise / -ies 49
sunscreen / -een 37
sunset / -et 44
sunshade / -ade 12
sunshine / -ine 55
sunspot / -ot 81
sunstroke / -oke 66
suntan / -an 18
suntrap / -ap 21
supercool / -ool 72
supersonic / -ick 46
superstar / -a 8
suppertime / -ime 54
support / -ort 79
suppose / -ows 85
supreme / -eam 30
surfboard / -oard 62
surname / -ame 18
surpass / -ass 24
surpassed / -ast 24
surprise / -ies 49
surprising / -ing 56
surrender / -ender 41
surround / -ound 82
survey / -ay 27
surveyed / -ade 12
survive / -ive 60
suspect / -ect 34
suspend / -end 41
suspense / -ence 40
suss / -us 96

swag / -ag 13
swam / -am 17
swan / -on 68
swank / -ank 21
swarm / -orm 78
swashbuckle / -uckle 88
swat / -ot 81
sway / -ay 27
swayed / -ade 12
sways / -aze 28
swear / -air 15
swearword / -urred 95
sweat / -et 44
sweatband / -and 19
sweatshirt / -urt 96
swede / -eed 36
sweep / -eep 38
sweet / -eat 32
sweetcorn / -orn 78
sweeter / -eater 33
sweetheart / -art 23
sweetshop / -op 75
swell / -ell 39
swept / -ept 42
swift / -ift 50
swig / -ig 50
swill / -ill 52
swim / -im 53
swimsuit / -ute 98
swine / -ine 55
swing / -ing 56
swingboat / -oat 63
swipe / -ipe 57
swirl / -url 94
swish / -ish 58
switch / -itch 60
switchback / -ack 10
switchbacks / -acks 11
swizz / -is 58
swoon / -oon 73
swoop / -oop 74
sword / -oard 62
swore / -ore 76
sworn / -orn 78
swot / -ot 81
swum / -um 90
swung / -ung 92
sycamore / -ore 76
sycamores / -ores 77
synagogue / -og 65
synonym / -im 53
syringe / -inge 56

t

tabby / -abby 8
table / -able 8
tablespoon / -oon 73
tackle / -ackle 10
tact / -act 11
tactic / -ick 46
tadpole / -ole 67
tag / -ag 13
tail / -ale 14
tailback / -ack 10
tailspin / -in 54
take / -ake 16
takeaway / -ay 27
tale / -ale 14
talk / -ork 78
tall / -all 17
tally / -alley 17
tambourine / -een 37
tame / -ame 18
tamper / -amper 18
tan / -an 18
tang / -ang 20
tangerine / -een 37
tangle / -angle 20
tank / -ank 21
tanned / -and 19
tantrum / -um 90
tap / -ap 21
tape / -ape 21
tar / -a 8
tarmac / -ack 10
tarred / -ard 22
tart / -art 23
task / -ask 23
taste / -aced 9
tastebud / -ud 88
tattoo / -oo 70
tattooed / -ude 88
tattoos / -use 96
tatty / -atty 26
taught / -ort 79
taut / -ort 79
tax / -acks 11
tea / -e 29
teabag / -ag 13
teacake / -ake 16
teacup / -up 93
team / -eam 30

123

teamwork / -urk	94	thesaurus / -us	96	thunderstruck / -uck	87	told / -old	66
teapot / -ot	81	these / -ees	38	Thursday / -ay	27	tomahawk / -ork	78
tear / -air	15	they / -ay	27	thus / -us	96	tomboy / -oy	86
tear / -ear	31	thick / -ick	46	thwack / -ack	10	tombstone / -one	69
teardrop / -op	75	thief / -eaf	30	thwacked / -act	11	tomcat / -at	24
tearful / -ul	90	thigh / -i	45	thwacks / -acks	11	tomorrow / -o	61
tearoom / -oom	73	thighbone / -one	69	thwart / -ort	79	ton / -un	92
tearstain / -ane	20	thighs / -ies	49	thyme / -ime	54	tone / -one	69
tease / -ees	38	thin / -in	54	Tibet / -et	44	tongue / -ung	92
teashop / -op	75	thing / -ing	56	tick / -ick	46	tonight / -ight	51
teaspoon / -oon	73	thingamabob / -ob	63	ticket / -it	59	too / -oo	70
teat / -eat	32	think / -ink	56	ticks / -icks	47	took / -ook	72
teatime / -ime	54	third / -urred	95	tick-tock / -ock	64	tool / -ool	72
technique / -eek	37	thirteen / -een	37	tick-tocks / -ocks	64	toolshed / -ed	35
tee / -e	29	this / -iss	58	tics / -icks	47	toot / -ute	98
tee-hee / -e	29	thorax / -acks	11	tide / -ide	48	toothache / -ake	16
teem / -eam	30	thorn / -orn	78	tie / -i	45	toothbrush / -ush	97
teen / -een	37	those / -ows	85	tied / -ide	48	toothpaste / -aced	9
teenage / -age	13	though / -o	61	tier / -ear	31	top / -op	75
teepee / -e	29	thought / -ort	79	ties / -ies	49	topknot / -ot	81
teepees / -ees	38	thrash / -ash	23	tiff / -iff	49	topsoil / -oil	65
teeter / -eater	33	thread / -ed	35	tigerskin / -in	54	tore / -ore	76
telephone / -one	69	threadbare / -air	15	tight / -ight	51	torment / -ent	41
telescope / -ope	75	threat / -et	44	tightrope / -ope	75	torn / -orn	78
televise / -ies	49	three / -e	29	tile / -ile	52	tornado / -o	61
tell / -ell	39	threesome / -um	90	tiled / -ild	52	toss / -oss	80
telltale / -ale	14	thresh / -esh	42	till / -ill	52	tot / -ot	81
ten / -en	40	threw / -oo	70	tilt / -ilt	53	touch / -uch	87
tend / -end	41	thrift / -ift	50	time / -ime	54	touchdown / -own	84
tender / -ender	41	thrill / -ill	52	timepiece / -eece	36	touchline / -ine	55
tennis / -iss	58	throat / -oat	63	timetable / -able	8	tough / -uff	89
tense / -ence	40	throb / -ob	63	timid / -id	47	tourist / -ist	58
tent / -ent	41	throes / -ows	85	tin / -in	54	tow / -o	61
terrapin / -in	54	throne / -one	69	tinfoil / -oil	65	toward / -oard	62
terrific / -ick	46	throng / -ong	69	tinge / -inge	56	towbar / -a	8
terrified / -ide	48	through / -oo	70	tint / -int	57	towed / -oad	62
terrifies / -ies	49	throughout / -out	83	tip / -ip	57	towel / -owl	84
terrify / -i	45	throw / -o	61	tiptoe / -o	61	tower / -ower	84
test / -est	43	thrown / -one	69	tiptoes / -ows	85	town / -own	84
textbook / -ook	72	throws / -ows	85	tire / -ire	57	townsfolk / -oke	66
than / -an	18	thrush / -ush	97	tissue / -oo	71	towrope / -ope	75
thank / -ank	21	thrust / -ust	97	tittle-tattle / -attle	26	tows / -ows	85
that / -at	24	thud / -ud	88	to / -oo	70	toy / -oy	86
thatch / -atch	24	thug / -ug	89	toad / -oad	62	toys / -oise	66
thaw / -ore	76	thumb / -um	90	toadstool / -ool	72	trace / -ace	9
thaws / -ores	77	thumbnail / -ale	14	toast / -ost	80	traced / -aced	9
their / -air	15	thumbprint / -int	57	today / -ay	27	track / -ack	10
them / -em	40	thump / -ump	91	toe / -o	61	tracked / -act	11
theme / -eam	30	thunder / -under	92	toenail / -ale	14	tracks / -acks	11
then / -en	40	thunderbolt / -olt	67	toes / -ows	85	tracksuit / -ute	98
there / -air	15	thunderclap / -ap	21	toffee / -e	29	trade / -ade	12
therefore / -ore	76	thundercloud / -oud	82	toffees / -ees	38	tragic / -ick	46
		thunderstorm / -orm	78	toil / -oil	65	trail / -ale	14

trailblaze / -aze	28	tropics / -icks	47
train / -ane	20	trot / -ot	81
traitor / -ator	26	troubadour / -ore	76
tra-la-la / -a	8	troubadours / -ores	77
tram / -am	17	trouble / -ubble	87
tramp / -amp	18	troublesome / -um	90
trampoline / -een	37	troupe / -oop	74
trance / -ance	19	trout / -out	83
tranquil / -ill	52	trowel / -owl	84
transatlantic / -antic	21	truce / -oose	74
transfer / -ur	94	truck / -uck	87
translate / -ate	25	truckload / -oad	62
translator / -ator	26	trudge / -udge	89
transmitter / -itter	60	true / -oo	71
transplants / -ance	19	trump / -ump	91
transport / -ort	79	trumpet / -it	59
trap / -ap	21	trunk / -unk	93
trapdoor / -ore	76	trust / -ust	97
trapdoors / -ores	77	try / -i	45
trapeze / -ees	38	tsar / -ar	8
trash / -ash	23	T-shirt / -urt	96
trawl / -all	17	tub / -ub	87
tray / -ay	27	tuck / -uck	87
trays / -aze	28	Tuesday / -ay	27
tread / -ed	35	tug / -ug	89
treadmill / -ill	52	tulip / -ip	57
treat / -eat	32	tum / -um	90
tree / -e	29	tumble / -umble	91
trees / -ees	38	tummy / -ummy	91
treetop / -op	75	tune / -oon	73
trek / -eck	33	turboprop / -op	75
trellis / -iss	58	Turk / -urk	95
tremendous / -us	96	turmoil / -oil	65
trench / -ench	40	turn / -urn	94
trend / -end	41	turnaround / -ound	82
tress / -ess	42	turnstile / -ile	52
trial / -ile	52	turntable / -able	8
triangle / -angle	20	turquoise / -oise	66
tribute / -ute	98	tusk / -usk	97
trice / -ice	46	tut-tut / -ut	97
trick / -ick	46	tutu / -oo	71
tricks / -icks	47	tu-whit tu-whoo / -oo	70
tried / -ide	48	twang / -ang	20
tries / -ies	49	tweak / -eek	37
trill / -ill	52	tweed / -eed	36
trim / -im	53	tweet / -eat	32
Trinidad / -ad	12	twice / -ice	46
trip / -ip	57	twiddle / -iddle	47
triplet / -it	59	twig / -ig	50
tripod / -od	65	twilight / -ight	51
trod / -od	65	twin / -in	54
trombone / -one	69	twine / -ine	55
troop / -oop	74	twinge / -inge	56

twirl / -url	94
twist / -ist	58
twit / -it	59
twitch / -itch	60
twitter / -itter	60
two / -oo	70
two-seater / -eater	33
twosome / -um	90
tycoon / -oon	73
type / -ipe	57
typhoon / -oon	73
tyre / -ire	57

u

UFO / -o	61
UFOs / -ows	85
umpteen / -een	37
unable / -able	8
unalike / -ike	51
unbend / -end	41
unbolt / -olt	67
unclear / -ear	31
uncoil / -oil	65
uncurl / -url	94
under / -under	92
underage / -age	13
underarm / -arm	23
undercut / -ut	97
underdog / -og	65
underfed / -ed	35
underfill / -ill	52
underfoot / -oot	74
underground / -ound	82
underhand / -and	19
underline / -ine	55
underlined / -ind	55
undermined / -ind	55
underpaid / -ade	12
underpass / -ass	24
underripe / -ipe	57
undersea / -e	29
understand / -and	19
understood / -ood	72
undertake / -ake	16
underwear / -air	15
underweight / -ate	25
undo / -oo	70
undone / -un	92
undress / -ess	42
undressed / -est	43

uneasy / -easy	32
unfair / -air	15
unfold / -old	66
unforeseen / -een	37
unfreeze / -ees	38
unfroze / -ows	85
unfurl / -url	94
unglue / -oo	71
unheard / -urred	95
unicorn / -orn	78
uniform / -orm	78
unimpressed / -est	43
unique / -eek	37
unite / -ight	51
universe / -urse	95
unjust / -ust	97
unkind / -ind	55
unknown / -one	69
unlace / -ace	9
unlaced / -aced	9
unlatch / -atch	24
unless / -ess	42
unlike / -ike	51
unload / -oad	62
unlock / -ock	64
unlocks / -ocks	64
unmade / -ade	12
unmask / -ask	23
unpack / -ack	10
unpacked / -act	11
unpacks / -acks	11
unpaid / -ade	12
unplug / -ug	89
unreal / -eal	30
unrest / -est	43
unripe / -ipe	57
unroll / -ole	67
unrolled / -old	66
unromantic / -antic	21
unscrew / -oo	70
unseen / -een	37
unsold / -old	66
unsound / -ound	82
unstable / -able	8
unstuck / -uck	87
unsung / -ung	92
untangle / -angle	20
unthread / -ed	35
untie / -i	45
untied / -ide	48
until / -ill	52
untold / -old	66
untrue / -oo	71

unwary / -airy	16	vat / -at	24
unwell / -ell	39	veer / -ear	31
unwind / -ind	55	vein / -ane	20
unwise / -ies	49	vent / -ent	41
unwrap / -ap	21	ventilator / -ator	26
unzip / -ip	57	venue / -oo	71
up / -up	93	verse / -urse	95
update / -ate	25	very / -erry	42
upend / -end	41	vest / -est	43
uphill / -ill	52	vet / -et	44
upkeep / -eep	38	vex / -ecks	34
upon / -on	68	vibrate / -ate	25
uppercut / -ut	97	video / -o	61
upright / -ight	51	videos / -ows	85
upriver / -iver	60	videotape / -ape	21
uproar / -ore	76	view / -oo	70
uproot / -ute	98	viewed / -ude	88
upset / -et	44	viewpoint / -oint	65
upshot / -ot	81	vigil / -ill	52
upstage / -age	13	vile / -ile	52
upstart / -art	23	vine / -ine	55
upstream / -eam	30	violin / -in	54
urn / -urn	95	VIP / -e	29
us / -us	96	virus / -us	96
use / -oose	74	visit / -it	59
use / -use	96	vitamin / -in	54
useful / -ul	90	vivid / -id	47
usherette / -et	44	volcano / -o	61
utmost / -ost	80	volcanoes / -ows	85
utter / -utter	98	vole / -ole	67
U-turn / -urn	94	volleyball / -all	17
		volt / -olt	67
		volunteer / -ear	31

vaccinate / -ate	25	voodoo / -oo	70
vaccine / -een	37	vote / -oat	63
vagabond / -ond	69	vouch / -ouch	81
vain / -ane	20	vow / -ow	83
valentine / -ine	55	vowed / -oud	82
valid / -id	47	vowel / -owl	84
valley / -alley	17	vroom / -oom	73
valley / -e	29		
value / -oo	71		
valued / -ude	88		
vampire / -ire	57		
van / -an	18		
vane / -ane	20		
vanish / -ish	58		
various / -us	96		
vary / -airy	16		
vast / -ast	24		

wade / -ade	12	wake / -ake	16
wag / -ag	13	wakeful / -ul	90
wage / -age	13	walk / -ork	78
wail / -ale	14	walkie-talkie / -e	29
waist / -aced	9	wall / -all	17
waistcoat / -oat	63	wallflower / -ower	84
wait / -ate	25	walnut / -ut	97
waiter / -ator	26	walrus / -us	96
		wan / -on	68
		wand / -ond	69
		wane / -ane	20
		war / -ore	76
		ward / -oard	62
		wardrobe / -obe	64
		warehouse / -ouse	83
		warlike / -ike	51
		warm / -orm	78
		wars / -ores	77
		warship / -ip	57
		wart / -ort	79
		wary / -airy	16
		wash / -osh	80
		waste / -aced	9
		wasteland / -and	19
		watchdog / -og	65
		watchful / -ul	90
		watchstrap / -ap	21
		watchtower / -ower	84
		waterborne / -orn	78
		watercress / -ess	42
		waterfall / -all	17
		waterski / -e	29
		watertight / -ight	51
		waterweed / -eed	36
		wave / -ave	27
		waveband / -and	19
		wax / -acks	11
		waxwork / -urk	94
		way / -ay	27
		ways / -aze	28
		we / -e	29
		weak / -eek	37
		wean / -een	37
		wear / -air	15
		weathercock / -ock	64
		weathervane / -ane	20
		weave / -eve	44
		website / -ight	51
		wed / -ed	35
		wedge / -edge	35
		Wednesday / -ay	27
		wee / -e	29
		weed / -eed	36

week / -eek	37
weekday / -ay	27
weekdays / -aze	28
weekender / -ender	41
weep / -eep	38
weigh / -ay	27
weighed / -ade	12
weight / -ate	25
welcome / -um	90
well / -ell	39
well-paid / -ade	12
went / -ent	41
wept / -ept	42
were / -ur	94
west / -est	43
westbound / -ound	82
wet / -et	44
wetsuit / -ute	98
whack / -ack	10
whacked / -act	11
whacks / -acks	11
whale / -ale	14
whaling / -ing	56
wham / -am	17
what / -ot	81
wheat / -eat	32
wheel / -eal	30
wheelbarrow / -o	61
wheelchair / -air	15
wheeze / -ees	38
wheezy / -easy	32
whelp / -elp	39
when / -en	40
where / -air	15
which / -itch	60
whiff / -iff	49
whiffed / -ift	50
while / -ile	52
whim / -im	53
whine / -ine	55
whined / -ind	55
whip / -ip	57
whiplash / -ash	23
whirl / -url	94
whirligig / -ig	50
whirlpool / -ool	72
whirlybird / -urred	95
whisk / -isk	58
white / -ight	51
whiteboard / -oard	62
whitewash / -osh	80
whizz / -is	58
who / -oo	70

Published 2014 by Bloomsbury Publishing Plc
50 Bedford Square, London WC1B 3DP
www.bloomsbury.com

Bloomsbury is a registered trademark of Bloomsbury Publishing Plc

Text copyright
© 2003 Pie Corbett and Ruth Thomson

First published 2003 by A & C Black

Designed by Rachel Hamdi and Holly Mann
Edited by Mary-Jane Wilkins
Illustrations by Sofie Forrester, Sarah Garson, Kate Pankhurst,
Holly Surplice and Sara Wilson

1 3 5 7 9 10 8 6 4 2

Thanks to Lilian Briggs for her advice.

A CIP record for this book is available from
the British Library.

ISBN 978-1-4729-1639-6

Typeset in New Contemporary Brush, Cosmos
and Stempel Garamond

Printed in China by Imago

This book is produced using paper that is made from wood grown in
managed, sustainable forests. It is natural, renewable and recyclable.
The logging and manufacturing processes conform to the environmental
regulations of the country of origin.

To view more of our titles, please visit:
www.bloomsbury.com

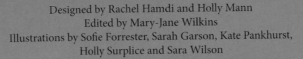
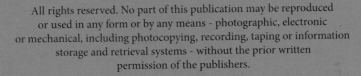
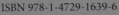